THE JEWISH QUARTERLY

The Jewish Quarterly is published four times a year
by The Jewish Quarterly Pty Ltd

Publisher: Morry Schwartz

ISBN 9781760645465 E-ISBN 9781743824245
ISSN 0449010X E-ISSN 23262516

Subscriptions 1 year print & digital (4 issues): £42 GBP | $56 USD | $74.99 AUD
1 year digital only: £25 GBP | $32 USD | $44.99 AUD. Payment may be made
by Mastercard or Visa. Includes postage and handling.

Subscribe online at jewishquarterly.com or email subscribe@jewishquarterly.com
Correspondence should be addressed to: The Editor, The Jewish Quarterly,
22–24 Northumberland Street, Collingwood VIC 3066 Australia
Phone +61 3 9486 0288 Email enquiries@jewishquarterly.com

The Jewish Quarterly is published under licence from the
Jewish Literary Trust Limited, which exercises a governance function.

UK Company Number: 01189861. UK Charity Commission Number: 268589.

Founding Editor: Jacob Sonntag.

Editor: Jonathan Pearlman. Associate Editor: Jo Rosenberg.
Publishing Coordinator: Noa Abrahams. Management: Elisabeth Young.
Design: John Warwicker and Tristan Main. Production: Marilyn de Castro.
Typesetting: Tristan Main.

Issue 261, August 2025

THE JEWISH QUARTERLY

Shameless

Exploiting the Holocaust

Tanya Gold is a British journalist who writes for *Harper's* magazine, *The Spectator*, the *Jewish Chronicle* and the *New York Times*. She won best feature writer at the British Press awards in 2010 and a Foreign Press Association award in 2015. She lives in west Cornwall.

The Jewish Quarterly is grateful for support from:

The Anglo–Jewish Association

The Exilarch's Foundation

The Polonsky Foundaton

Shameless

Exploiting the Holocaust

Tanya Gold

"Is this all that will be remembered of the Event?"

—Elie Wiesel

Last spring my sister sent me a photograph of a novel called *The Stable Boy of Auschwitz: A Heartbreaking True Story of Courage and Survival.* I stared at the photograph, and I thought: who is this novel for? What does it serve?

I was disgusted but not surprised. There is a glut of Shoah popular culture nowadays, and it is self-perpetuating. The Shoah can be a creation myth or a punchline. Marvel's *X-Men* (2000) begins in Auschwitz; *X-Men: Apocalypse* (2016) ends there. Bridget Jones's mother begs her not to walk around 1990s London "looking like someone from Auschwitz, darling". As I write, Wendy Holden's new novel, *The Teacher of Auschwitz*, has just been published, and *The Boys from Brazil*, the 1978 Jewsploitation film (Hitler lives, as multiple clones!) is being remade for fools. The Shoah is everywhere in popular culture but, as it really was, it is nowhere. There is too much of it, and too little. It is spoken of ceaselessly but it is almost never faced.

Until 7 October 2023, I knew this, and I didn't care. Let people watch *X-Men*'s Magneto raze Auschwitz; let them reanimate the Wannsee Conference as an English-style tea party in *Conspiracy* (2001). (In this film the genocidaire Reinhard Heydrich says of Schubert's Quintet in C major: "The adagio will tear your heart out." No doubt.) I have my own Shoah culture as memorial: the works of survivors Primo Levi, Elie Wiesel and Tadeusz Borowski; the testimony of the *Sonderkommando* Zalmen Gradowski and the historian of the Warsaw Ghetto, Emanuel Ringelblum; two incalculably tender novels by the British writer Martin Amis; Cynthia Ozick's short story "The Shawl" (1980); and a few films, including *The Pawnbroker* (1964), *Son of Saul* (2015) and the immense documentary *Shoah* (1985) by Claude Lanzmann. Before he died in 2018, Lanzmann said: "*Shoah* is the construction of a memory. And the act of transmitting is all that matters. There was no reality to film. It had to be created. *Shoah* is the abolition of all distance between past and present. *Shoah* shows eyes that saw. I wanted to make this film to resurrect them and kill them a second time so we could die with them, and they wouldn't die alone."

After 7 October 2023, when the murder of Israeli Jews was celebrated on the streets of Europe, I thought I had been wrong to dismiss the glut as harmless. I re-read and rewatched the famous works that are apparently about the Shoah: the blockbuster novels and films that non-Jews read and watch; the literary novels pseudo-intellectuals praise. And I understood, for the first time, the connection between the emphasis, glibness and heartlessness of these works, and the existence – the continuation – of the hatred that created the Shoah. Because they amount to, by instalments – sometimes subconsciously, sometimes not – the erasure of the Jew from the Shoah, and his own history. Patterns emerge in these works: Jews are stripped of Jewish character and hinterland, so the reason for their murder is obscured; the perpetrator is an object of fascination, often glamour; the Jew is replaced by the non-Jew to create a non-Jewish tragedy to rebuke the Jew himself; sometimes the Jew is the perpetrator. Inside these cumulative fictions the Jew becomes, as he has always been, a mythical being who cannot be loved or mourned: you cannot love – or harm – an idea. And of the overwhelmingly Yiddish-speaking Jewish nation that is gone there is almost nothing.

We read Anne's book, which is so full of self-knowledge, but it is we who know her ending

It began with Anne Frank.

Last year a friend sent me a photograph of a child, the daughter of an acquaintance of hers. The child was reading *The Diary of a Young Girl*, her head bent to the page. This was code. It was supposed to tell me that my friend, who has remained silent on the anti-Israel protests in our country since October 2023, understood the meaning of the Shoah, and of my fear. This – sending me the photograph – was her speech, and her consolation. It angered me, and I wanted to reply: why are you sending me a photograph of a living Christian child reading a book by the world's most famous dead Jewish child? Haven't you read Cynthia Ozick's essay on Anne Frank?

Anne Frank was a writer, and, as writers do, she invented herself. But she did not get to keep herself. The attic on Prinsengracht in Amsterdam, where Anne lived from 1942 to 1944, was, among other things, a crucible for her gift. Her talent grew faster than it would have outside. Great writers need great subjects. Anne had that, and she died for it: what can be more poignant? We read her book, which is so full of self-knowledge, but it is we who know her ending; she does not. And so, a cult arose around her, and I have always thought there was something controlling, even repulsive, about it. To the cult, Anne is an object of fascination and projection: a ghost, a German-Jewish child who does not know she is dead.

If she was lonely in life, now she has millions of friends: more poignancy. And these friends learn, from her terror and death at fifteen, a hopeful message. They go to her for consolation: to learn that the world is still a kindly place. The most famous line in the diary – her inspirational mantra, if you will – is: "In spite of everything I still believe that people are truly good at heart." It is the pull-out quote on the Amazon page. It appears on t-shirts. But, as the writer Dara Horn notes, "Frank wrote about people being 'truly good at heart' before meeting people who weren't." Anne also wrote of rage and anguish but there are no t-shirts that say "Let the end come, however cruel" or "We are Jews in chains". Perhaps they should. But Shoah culture is a mirror, and people see what they desire: forgiveness from Anne, because she forgives us, and an active absolution by reading her. "I want to go on living even after my death!" Anne wrote in 1944. The reader can give her what she wants.

The diary is relatable and, through editing and multiple films, has become more relatable still. The Franks were assimilated, irreligious Jews: Anne is the Everychild, and her Jewishness is stripped away to an afterthought, a whim even. Perhaps it is the non-Jewish representations of the Franks – a 2009 version had a practising Christian and a Scot playing Anne's parents, baffled portraits of anxiety – but I would not be surprised if soon there were a version in which Anne is not Jewish at all but has converted to Jedi; works for the UN or Christian Dior; lives in Hope, Arkansas, or on Mars. Her book, as it now stands, is not even Anne Frank Versus the Nazis. It is Anne Frank Versus Her Mother (Edith), who vexed her. (This may be so, but, in Auschwitz in 1944, Edith saved her bread to give to her daughters, should she ever see them again. She didn't.) Because the troubling mother part – well, any girl can relate. The diary is almost a common tale of anguished adolescence. Almost.

It is not a Shoah story, but a pre-Shoah story at best: the attic is breached off-page. Anne's gifts are so great – her writing is luminous, it is real – that she allows us to imagine her still alive, and I think this is another reason why people read her: to imagine that she did not die. In Cracow you can buy wooden Jews from gift shops and market stalls. They are 10 centimetres high, called Lucky Jews, and they replace the Jews that have gone. They are toys and they are malleable. I have never seen a female one but when I think of Anne Frank, I think of them.

Because we know Anne is dead, and she doesn't, Cynthia Ozick says in her excoriating 1997 *New Yorker* piece on the cult of Anne Frank, the diary "cannot count as Anne Frank's story. A story may not be said to be a story if the end is missing." Without the end, the story has "been bowdlerized, distorted, transmuted, traduced, reduced; it has been infantilized, Americanized, homogenized, sentimentalized; falsified, kitschified, and, in fact, blatantly and arrogantly denied." Anne's "dread came to be described as hope, her terror as courage, her prayers of despair as inspiring". The result? "A deeply truth-telling work has been turned into an instrument of partial truth, surrogate truth, or anti-truth."

When Anne's father, Otto Frank, returned to Amsterdam after the war, Miep Gies, who had helped hide the family, gave him the diary. He edited it to remove Anne's fury. A similar thing happened to Elie Wiesel's *Night* (144 pages when it was published in French; 862 pages in the original Yiddish); even Primo Levi removed Jewish references from *If This Is a Man* (1947) to make it more relatable. Otto removed Anne's musings on her body, her rage towards her mother, her hatred for Germans, some of her Judaism. He was a traumatised Jew, practised in compliance. Ozick believes him uncomfortable with fury, even if his family was all dead: it is also possible his amendments were a normal father's rejection of his daughter's subversion. Instead of allowing her fury, Otto sanctified Anne, so she would be loved at last, though on the terms of others.

In the original German translation in 1950, by Anneliese Schütz, the reader could be soothed by certain word choices and omissions. One of Anne's house rules in the attic was "It is necessary to speak softly at all times. Only the language of civilized people may be spoken, thus no German." In Schütz's translation, this became "all civilized languages ... but softly!" "Heroism in the war or when confronting the Germans" became "heroism in the war and in the struggle against oppression". "There is no greater hostility than exists between Germans and Jews" became "there is no greater hostility in the world than between *these* Germans and Jews!" (My italics.) But, as Ozick surmises, the diary should not be soothing. This was never Anne's intent.

This is everywhere in Shoah culture: the soothing away of the truth. When Claude Lanzmann interviewed Polish witnesses for *Shoah*, the translator changed "*Żydki*", the pejorative "little Yid", to "Jews". In Israel, the translator changed the words of Antek Zuckerman, the deputy commander of the Warsaw Ghetto Uprising. "I started drinking after the war when I climbed up onto that huge tomb" became "I started drinking after the war … It was very difficult". But Lanzmann, who grew up in occupied France, got the truth from Zuckerman: he lived for it. ("My homeland is my film," he declared of his vocation.) Zuckerman told him, "Claude, if you could lick my heart, it would poison you." There are no famous books about Antek Zuckerman, because no one would read them.

Anne Frank, who died because she was a Jew, became a paragon of universal love

But Anne Frank is useful and pleasing: ever the fate of a girl. Her diary was published in America in 1952; in 1955 it became a sanitised, Pulitzer Prize–winning play by Frances Goodrich and Albert Hackett, authors of the film *It's a Wonderful Life*. The play includes the line: "We're not the only people that've had to suffer. There've always been people that've had to … sometimes one race … sometimes another." And: "If all men are good, there was never an Auschwitz." The first denies the exceptionalism of the Shoah within an artwork that purports to be about it; the second suggests the Shoah is potentially theoretical. Anne Frank, who died because she was a Jew, became a paragon of universal love, the thing she least embodies.

That is why it is common for people to hold placards at anti-Israel marches that purloin her image for the cause of Palestine, and why the Anne Frank House in Amsterdam forbade a Jewish employee from openly wearing a yarmulke in 2018: meet Anne the ghostly political activist. You can buy, if you wish, a canvas shopping bag with a quotation from the diary, "How wonderful it is that no one has to wait even a minute to start gradually changing the world." *How wonderful.* What a thing to say in relation to Anne Frank. *How wonderful.* After six months the museum relented and allowed the Jew to wear his yarmulke. It was, as Dara Horn wrote, "a rather long time for the Anne Frank House to ponder whether it was a good idea to force a Jew into hiding".

The critics loved the 1955 play, because in the end it delivered the audience to safety. "Anne is not going to her death; she is going to leave a dent on life, and let death take what's left," said the critic Walter Kerr, a sentence so idiotic I am amazed he allowed himself to write it. *A dent?* Anne Frank left *a dent on life?* "We see in Anne Frank's fate," a German drama critic wrote, "our own fate – the tragedy of human existence per se." The Anne Frank cult is a monument to deception ("our own fate"), minimalisation, and self-absorption posing as sympathy. You cannot learn the universal lesson of the Shoah, which for me is an edict to love the stranger, if you have not first learned the particular lesson: the victims were Jews. The diary is a fine piece of testimony if taken as that: a piece of testimony. As a world-famous cultural artefact, it is something else: erasure of the rest.

As I write, there are twenty-seven films about Anne Frank, slightly fewer than in the Marvel Cinematic Universe. I watch the original, based on the play: it is all that I can bear. *The Diary of Anne Frank*, 1959 – a Twentieth Century-Fox production – is formal and stylised. Perhaps it is the cinematography, or the fact it was written by the author of *Father of the Bride*, but I think Otto should have been played by Spencer Tracy. It opens to the sound of church bells. It is wrapped in church bells, but it doesn't feel like metaphor. It feels like wedding bells. It opens with not–Spencer Tracy (Joseph Schildkraut) climbing the stairs above the spice factory after the war to find that "Anne's diary is where she left it". The diary is safe, and that is what matters: the preservation of the inspirational mantra. And, for a while, so is Anne, played by Millie Perkins with a singsong American accent. (I understand: German would be alienating.) In the diaries Anne had an intensity: you can read it in the polish of her sentences; in her love for Otto and her fury with Edith; in her negotiations between "good" and "bad" Anne. You can read it everywhere. Perkins does not show such intensity. I think she was chosen because she had dark hair, and she is no more a convincing Jewish artist than Mrs Maisel. Her mother, Edith, is played by Gusti Huber, an Austrian star of Nazi cinema.

Somehow, having a replete Austrian who worked under the aegis of Joseph Goebbels play a terrified Jewish mother is not tasteless for the Frank cult. In fact, she is rather good.

In the film, Anne is an ordinary American teenager in extraordinary circumstances. "With all the boys in the world," she asks, referring to Peter van Daan, "how did I have to get locked up with him?" Where is Anne's seriousness? Where is her Jewishness? There is a menorah Mrs Frank looks at anxiously, as if it is something to fear, and that's pretty much it. Instead, we hear about Mrs van Daan's sexual boundaries, and the cracks and bangs of the attic, because this is a haunted house in which the eight Jews are trying "to hold on to our ideals". (Not their Judaism, of course. Their *ideals*.) At one point Anne says, "If I say too much, I will hurt people's feelings." (Now that is true.) "We don't need the Nazis to destroy us," says Otto when the families quarrel, "we are destroying ourselves." Really? Is Crematorium V in the attic?

What we do get is a love story: because it is relatable. What else? Anne and Peter talk about heaven and hell and purgatory – more church bells – and kiss to the sound of a happy ending. (The score is overwhelming.) It is monstrously, laughably jarring. They don't show the arrest because that would be too frightening (for the viewer): nor do we see the journey to Westerbork, or to Auschwitz, where Edith and the van Daans died and Anne saw gypsy girls being taken to the gas chambers (as a survivor recounted to a German researcher); or the journey to Bergen-Belsen, where Anne and her sister, Margot, died of typhus as the war was ending. This is as much Kansas as Auschwitz, more fantasy than testimony, and that is surely the purpose.

The film ends with the mantra – the t-shirt, the fridge magnet, the pin! – *In spite of everything I still believe that people are really good at heart*. Otto reads this from the diary and says, "She puts me to shame." This is a warning against rage, grief even, using the words of a girl who never had the opportunity to amend them, being dead. It is, consciously or not, a rebuke.

Philip Roth understood Anne Frank's artistic tragedy. He tried to rescue her in the 1979 novel *The Ghost Writer*. It is about Nathan Zuckerman, a young post-war Jewish writer, alienated from his father after writing a brutal story of Jewish family strife. Here, during a snowstorm, Zuckerman spends an eerie night in the rural home of Emmanuel Isidore Lonoff, a Russian-Jewish refugee and novelist. For Zuckerman, Lonoff's fiction is "a response to the same burden of exclusion and confinement that still

Anne has no value for the world if living; dead, she is useful

weighed upon the lives of those who had raised me, and that had informed our relentless household obsession with the status of the Jews". He calls Lonoff "the Jew who got away" – materially and emotionally – but he isn't. No one is. Lonoff's "thwarted, secretive, imprisoned souls" remind Zuckerman of the "unmurdered remnant of European Jewry" now in Palestine. It is not a restful evening.

Lonoff has a young house guest: Amy Bellette. She is cataloguing his papers for Harvard. "There she was, hair dark and profuse, eyes pale – grey or green – and with a high prominent oval forehead that looked like Shakespeare's". She has "a faint foreign accent" and her costume "seems like a little girl's". Mrs Lonoff, deranged by her husband's isolation, begs Lonoff to leave her for Amy.

> "Because I cannot live another moment as your jailer! Your nobility is eating away the last thing that is left! You are a monument and can take it and take it – but I'm down to nothing, darling, and I can't. Chuck me out! Please, now, before your goodness and your wisdom kill us both!"

Mrs Lonoff is the witness to a writer's life: she lives with Lonoff's detachment, his pointlessness – what have words done for Jews? – his anxiety. "It takes three months for him just to get used to a new brand of *soap*."

Early on, there is a clue to what will unfold. Zuckerman and his mother discuss the play *The Diary of Anne Frank*.

Zuckerman: "I didn't see it. I read the book. Everybody read the book."

His mother: "But you liked it, didn't you?"

Zuckerman: "That's not the issue. How can you dislike it?"

Through Zuckerman, Roth marvels at Anne Frank:

> It's like watching an accelerated film of a foetus sprouting a face, watching her mastering things. Suddenly she's discovering reflection, suddenly there's portraiture, character sketches, suddenly there's a long intricate eventful happening so beautifully recounted it seems to have gone through

a dozen drafts. And no poisonous notion of being interesting or serious. She just is.

The night in the snowstorm, camping in Lonoff's study, Zuckerman is charged by Lonoff to write a story, and Zuckerman chooses this: he imagines that Amy Bellette, Lonoff's "femme fatale", is really Anne Frank grown up. He hears her in the room upstairs, trying to seduce Lonoff but failing, because Lonoff is dead in his way. "Oh, Manny, would it kill you just to kiss my breasts? Is that dreamy, too? Would it cause the death of anyone if you just did that?" Anne lives!

"Oh, Manny," she tells him. "Their Anne Frank is theirs; I want to be your Anne Frank. Child Martyr and Holy Saint isn't a position I'm really qualified for anymore. They wouldn't even have me, not as I am, longing for somebody else's husband, begging him to leave his loyal wife to run off with a girl half his age." When she had met Lonoff she told him that "of all the Jewish writers, from Franz Kafka to E.I. Lonoff, she was the most famous. But only" – here Roth rebukes the cult for its insincerity and morbidity – "if she were believed to be dead."

Anne has no value for the world if living; dead, she is useful. It is Christianity, obvious and absolute. (Anne means "grace".) I didn't read Anne Frank when I was a girl. I sensed it was not for me. I read Elie Wiesel, who wrote, in *Night* (1956), the closest thing we have to a sequel to Anne's diary. He was fifteen when he was deported from Sighet, Romania, to Auschwitz, where his mother and sister were murdered. I memorised this quotation:

Never shall I forget that night, the first night in camp, that turned my life into one long night seven times sealed. Never shall I forget that smoke. Never shall I forget the small faces of the children whose bodies I saw transformed into smoke under a silent sky. Never shall I forget those flames that consumed my faith forever. Never shall I forget the nocturnal silence that deprived me for all eternity of the desire to live. Never shall I forget those moments that murdered my God and my soul and turned my dreams to ashes. Never shall I forget those things, even were I condemned to live as long as God Himself.

Wiesel gives no consolation, for he got none.

When a child is hanged: "'For God's sake, where is God?' And from within me, I heard a voice answer: 'Where He is? This is where – hanging here from this gallows ...' That night, the soup tasted of corpses."

Dead, Anne is more pliant than Wiesel, and available. In *The Ghost Writer* Zuckerman's imagined Anne tells Lonoff that people visit her attic: "They looked at the open pages of her secret diary. That was her handwriting, they whispered, those are her words." "They wept for me," said Amy, "they pitied me; they prayed for me; they begged my forgiveness. I was the incarnation of the millions of unlived years robbed from the murdered Jews. It was too late to be alive now. I was a saint." She had written, "without meaning to or trying to, a book with the force of a masterpiece to make people finally see ... What would happen when people had finally seen? The only realistic answer was Nothing."

She knows her power: she is an undead dead Jew, but she is not too Jewish. She is Jesus Christ of the Attic.

> To expect the great callous and indifferent world to care about the child of a pious, bearded father living under the sway of the rabbis and the rituals – that was pure folly. To ordinary people it probably would seem that they had invited disaster by stubbornly repudiating everything modern and European – not to say Christian. But the family of Otto Frank, that would be another matter!

If, before, she could write, "people are truly good at heart", Zuckerman's Anne Frank could no longer sing in praise of them. "An axe was what she really wanted, not print."

Shoah fiction is filled with fantasy: moral and immoral; agonised and self-satisfied; yearning and deadening. Even witnesses bend to it: Lanzmann's Polish interviewees "seemed pleased to have found a stranger curious about a past they remembered with extraordinary exactness, yet one that they spoke of as if it were legend". But few are as shrewd as Roth's. "When the sleeve of her coat fell back, I of course saw that there was no scar on her forearm. No scar; no book; no Pim [Otto]. No, the loving father who must be relinquished for the sake of his child's art was not hers; he was mine."

The Ghost Writer is about, among many things, morbid unseeing. I think it is a tribute to Anne as I read her in her diary – and I can imagine her crawling over E.I. Lonoff; I cheer for her – and a musing on how speechless artists can feel when faced with the Shoah, if they have integrity. Roth had great gifts but, here, manifested in Lonoff, they are hollow. "I turn sentences around," he says. "That's my life. I write a sentence and then I turn it around. Then I look at it and I turn it around again. Then I have lunch."

There are two postscripts to the Anne Frank discussion: a libel and a truth. In 2022 Rosemary Sullivan, a Canadian poet, published *The Betrayal of Anne Frank: A Cold Case Investigation*, naming Arnold van den Bergh, a Jew, as her betrayer. The conclusion was irresistible: the Jews murdered *our* Anne Frank. They murdered themselves. It was bad fiction within bad fiction. And it felt inevitable. Real historians disputed Sullivan's findings, and the publishing house withdrew it. I thought of Amy Bellette's axe.

Then, in 2023, the memoir of Hannah Pick-Goslar, Anne's friend, was posthumously published: *My Friend Anne Frank*. Hannah was deported from Amsterdam to Westerbork, the Dutch transit camp. On 27 November 1943 Anne recorded a dream she'd had about Hannah, "clothed in rags", her face "thin and worn", as she begged Anne "to rescue me from this hell".

Hannah saw Anne in Bergen-Belsen in 1945. By this time, Anne was dying in a tent and was, Hannah writes:

So diminished, so entirely changed. "They took my hair," she said, her voice still full of disbelief. I felt the sting of her indignation. Her silky dark hair. She was forever brushing it, experimenting with curlers; it was her favourite feature.

And she was freezing, she told me, dressed only in rags. Margot was sick with typhus, too ill to move from bed, she reported. She told me the terrible news that her parents were dead. [In fact, Otto lived.] "Surely gassed to death," she said. She had seen the curls of crematorium smoke. "I have no one," she said.

Hannah threw food over the fence that separated them.

But then came terrible screams. It was Anne crying out from the other side. I heard a brief argument and footsteps of someone running away. "Anne, what happened? What's going on?" "A woman has caught it and won't give it to me!" Anne screamed. She was sobbing. Her cries were so loud I could tell she was convulsing with tears.

When Hannah returned, Anne was gone.

After the war Otto found a young Jewish woman, Lin Brilleslijper, who had met Anne and Margot in Bergen-Belsen. She called them "a pair of frozen birds". "Lin," Hannah writes, "said that Margot died first, after rising from her bunk but then crashing to the ground, followed shortly afterwards by a now completely hopeless and hallucinating Anne. Lin and her sister were the ones who discovered their bodies and together they carried them to one of the mass graves for burial." I wept when I read this. The happy omissions of the Anne Frank cult did not prepare me for the reality of her death any more than the shining lucidity of her diary, but here it is: Ozick's authentic ending, the truth.

Years later Hannah wrote: "I was fascinated that strangers were reading Anne's words. I can't remember anyone asking me about my experiences in the war." Perhaps Hannah, being alive, wasn't enough to be the object of a cult? Anne, though, is settled as a fictional creature, like Tinkerbell: if you believe in her, she lives. As G.K. Chesterton wrote, "I never said it was always wrong to enter fairyland, I only said it was always dangerous."

If Anne Frank gives us a Shoah without death, Oskar Schindler gives us a Shoah without Jews. He is multiple. There is the real Schindler, who died in Jerusalem in 1974 and is buried on Mount Zion. There is the Schindler of the people he saved – the so-called *Schindlerjuden*, a name I pause on because it speaks of possession. There is the Schindler of Thomas Keneally's 1982 novel *Schindler's Ark*, and the Schindler of Steven Spielberg's 1993 film *Schindler's List*: the most enduring, and beautiful, Schindler.

I watched the film numbly, as non-Jews ate popcorn around me. When I see it now, I cannot believe how much it reminds me of Golden Age cinema. What beautiful suits! No wonder the *New Yorker*'s film critic Pauline Kael hated *Shoah*, calling it "a long moan" that "closes your mind". Cinema ruined Kael's sensibilities, immunised her to reality. Spielberg changed reality by finessing it: it is his gift, and his curse, and I wonder if he knows it. I suspect he did, and decided to atone for it: in 1994 he founded the USC Shoah Foundation to gather testimony from survivors. But first this.

When we meet Schindler, he is wearing a tuxedo: a tango is playing. This is a nightclub, Kraków, 1939. Schindler is irresistible. Nazis love him; soon Jews will too. Schindler the archetype, the saviour: the bridge between. The maître d'hôtel is played by Branko Lustig, a Shoah survivor who co-produced the film, but most viewers will not know it. Still, Lustig's whisper in Schindler's ear, promising to please the Nazis Schindler wants to bribe, is exquisite. Lustig knew real Nazis: his own father had been the maître d'hôtel in Osijek Café Central, in Yugoslavia. But forget Lustig. He is at the edges, and he leaves to pour the drinks. You only look at Schindler (Liam Neeson) here to profit from the war. He seems to be modelled on Victor Laszlo of *Casablanca*: he has the same disarming, boyish quality, and his clothes are as fine. His Nazi pin shines.

Schindler's story is about a non-Jew and life: a redemption story

Schindler was a member of the Nazi Party, and he worked for German military intelligence. This is the story of a Nazi rescuer, not a Jew, or even many Jews. People love tales of rescue but, as Dara Horn writes, there are so few – 30,000 rescuers from a pre-war population of 300 million – they could be a rounding error. A Shoah story, if it is honest, must be about Jews and death. What else can be it about? Schindler's story is about a non-Jew and life: a redemption story, and the perfect piece of popular Shoah culture.

Schindler's List is less the invention of Thomas Keneally or Steven Spielberg than of a Polish Jew called Poldek Pfefferberg, whom Schindler saved. Pfefferberg is the real teller of Schindler's story, and he filled it with love. He filled it with all the love he had left: he'd lost almost one hundred members of his family. His intent – to honour Schindler – was noble. Pfefferberg understood the Shoah perfectly. Most do not and will not.

Thomas Keneally is an Australian novelist who had trained for the Catholic priesthood. In October 1980 he was in Beverly Hills and in need of a new briefcase. He stood outside the Handbag Studio. "I hesitated," Keneally wrote, "always a nervous shopper. But the shopkeeper soon appeared beside me, having stepped out from within." It was Poldek Pfefferberg: Schindler's Otto Frank, his myth maker.

"He had a stocky Slavic look ... a barrel chest, powerful arms, a wrestler's neck. There was a glitter of fraternal amusement in his eyes. Even then I perceived that he had dealt in markets beyond my knowing."

Pfefferberg said, "So it's 105 degrees out here and you don't want to come into my air-conditioned store. Do you think I'll eat you?" In a way, he did. When he learned Keneally was a novelist, Pfefferberg said, "I know a wonderful story. It's not a story for Jews but for everyone. I was saved, and my wife was saved, by a Nazi. So, although he's a Nazi, to me he's Jesus Christ. To me he is God."

The story is astounding: the problem is not in its telling, but in how it obscures other, more representative, stories about the Shoah. In 1939 Schindler bought an enamel factory in Kraków called Emalia. To staff it, he bought Jews from the SS. He treated them well and, as the Russians advanced in 1944, he moved them to Moravia to make shells for the German army. At the armistice, he persuaded the SS not to murder his workers, and he departed from Moravia with a ring inscribed by them in Hebrew: "He who saves a single life saves the world entire." It's both a beautiful line, and a lie: nine-tenths of Polish Jewry died in the Shoah. He also had a letter, in Hebrew, naming what he had done. He was picked up by the Americans, showed the letter to a rabbi travelling with them, and was feted.

Schindler had that mesmerising thing – duality. Pfefferberg's wife, Misia, told Keneally: "Oskar was a god. But Oskar was *Oskar* as well. He was very tall, and women loved him." He slept with German SS girls and Polish secretaries; he made his wife, Emilie, co-habit with his mistress and "drank cognac like water"; even female *Schindlerjuden* desired him. Keneally decided Schindler was "a ruined Catholic hedonist" manifesting "a dancing-on-the-lip-of-hell exuberance. As a struggling Catholic myself," he writes, "I had some time for fellows like Oskar." Everyone did. There are no famous novels about Raoul Wallenberg, rescuer of Hungarian Jewish children, or Józef and Wiktoria Ulma of Markowa, Poland, murdered alongside their seven children for hiding Jews. Schindler was bewitching, and he had an antagonist to meet him: Amon Goeth, "that highly placed sensualist", commandant of Płaszów, and seller of Jews. "Oskar's dark brother" was "the berserk and fanatic executioner Oskar might, by some unhappy reversal of his appetites, have become". And that's the story: not Wiesel's nocturnal silence and endless grief, but moral jeopardy for the non-Jew. What choices, as the introductory documentary film in the Auschwitz Museum asks in voice-over, will you make? Are you Schindler or Goeth?

In *Schindler's Ark*, Oskar dazzles: "a minor god of deliverance, double-faced – in the Greek manner – as any small god, endowed with all the human vices, many-handed, subtly powerful, capable of bringing gratuitous but secure salvation". He chain-smoked, "as ever. But it was composed chain smoking." He was "sleekly handsome in the style of the film stars George Sanders and Curt Jurgens". He was "a provider of outrageous salvation" but could "drink with the devil and adjust the balance of evil over a tumbler of cognac". Goeth, meanwhile, "claimed to be a poet" but, "after only an hour's sleep, he'd be on the balcony, infantry rifle in hand, ready to shoot any dilatory prisoners". Goeth "had been plagued with insomnia for two years now". (We will have more on Nazi health problems later: they are a Shoah culture trope.) Thanks to Schindler, "Amon had given up, for the time being at least, arbitrarily murdering people."

It is an odd novel, dual as Schindler was, and as Pfefferberg was. In parts it is overwritten melodrama pleading for seriousness, with sentences like: "History itself seemed to have gone malignant" and "This winter night, it is both early days and late days for Herr Schindler's practical engagement in the salvage of certain human lives."

There is, amid the story of a god gambling for Jews, valuable testimony. In Kraków, Keneally notes, Jews revived the practice of lengthening the foreskin to conceal their Jewishness. Artur Rosenzweig, the chairman of the Kraków Judenrat, "when asked in June to make a list of thousands for deportation, had placed his own name, his wife's, his daughter's at the top". Pfefferberg had barely changed since the war, when he was "an experienced prisoner ... [who] prepared himself for anything".

Even so, the key line in the novel is: "The list is an absolute good. The list is life. All round its cramped margins lies the gulf." It does not touch the gulf.

The film is better than the book, and less moral. It bounds along with Schindler's insatiable optimism. He is Tigger in hell, floating in a sea of Hennessy and Dom Pérignon, ever in motion, and this feels wrong to me. Nothing in authentic Shoah memory moves forward: it is always eastern Europe in wartime. And, watching it, I cannot forget, because Spielberg will not let me forget, that Schindler enjoyed the war. How is this glut of pleasure a real Shoah film? "The peace would never exalt him as had the war," Keneally writes. All his exultation is here, on the *Spielberg has played with antisemites before and since, surely an act of control* screen: when he pulls Itzhak Stern off the train to Auschwitz or, in scorching heat, sprays water at cattle cars filled with Jews, or slaps a child to stop a Nazi shooting him, you rejoice with him. *One more life! German Hotties Save the World (Entire)!*

It is true that Jewish anguish is shown, that the liquidation of the ghetto is barely watchable. But it is a film of elusion. According to Keneally, survivors told Spielberg the actors were too well dressed and too well fed: "they knew that if he reproduced the reality of their camp life, the viewer would be appalled and alienated". And I can't forgive Spielberg for casting Ralph Fiennes, the most beautiful actor of his generation, as Goeth. The real Goeth looked nothing like Fiennes – he looked like a dusty pudding – but Spielberg said he saw "sexual evil" in Fiennes's eyes. Is *antisemitism* not evil enough? I watch this film and I think, or rather, know: plenty of credulous women will imagine they would enjoy being Amon Goeth's maid.

Spielberg has played with antisemites before and since, surely an act of control. He invented the easily thwarted, undangerous cartoon Nazi in the Indiana Jones franchise; and in *The Fabelmans* (2022), the retelling of his baffling Jewish childhood in Arizona, there is a clue to his glamorisation of Goeth. In this film, Spielberg's avatar is Sammy Fabelman, who is bullied for his Jewishness by a boy at school named Logan. In response, Sammy makes a film of Logan playing sports, transforming him into a god. Logan, wounded by the fiction, asks Fabelman: "What's wrong with you?" "All I did," Sammy replies, "was hold the camera and it saw what it saw." Logan protests: "You made me look like this golden kind of thing." Sammy shouts, "I wanted you to be nice to me for five minutes. Or – I did it to make my movie better. I don't know why I did it. I have a monkey at home that's smarter than you. I made you look like you can fly!"

Sammy Fabelman was hurt, and he made evil beautiful, because he had no power to do anything else. It's passive-aggressive and self-hating, and perhaps a plea for meaning: let the cause of the pain be more interesting than it is. Flying Nazis.

The best scenes in *Schindler's List* are at the edges, where the Jews are. The history and literature teacher at the selection for factory workers, who asks if culture is: "Not essential?" Seconds later he is a metal polisher, looking at a metal press with wonder. The child who, recruited to work in the factory, tells Schindler, "It's an honour to work for such a great company." (Schindler, ever courteous, replies: "It's an honour to have you.") The Jewish child in the ghetto police, initially blowing a whistle with glutinous self-importance, but, on seeing the girl he loves, cries, "Hide, hide!" And Itzhak Stern (played by Ben Kingsley), who is the best character in the film because he is the only one in a Shoah film. Stern is a Jewish hero of a particular kind: a Leo Bloom of *The Producers*, a man who does the books. Schindler made money when Stern ran his business for him; after the war he floundered. Schindler gives him a glass of cognac to drink. Stern looks at it as if he does not know what it is.

In the film, Pfefferberg is cut back, and the two best scenes in the book do not appear at all. In the first, the Jewish violinist Henry Rosner fiddles an SS officer to death during a party. The officer wants to hear "Gloomy Sunday", "a syrupy love ballad in which a boy is about to commit suicide for love". Henry considers: "God, if I have the power, maybe this son of a bitch will kill himself." The magic worked. "The guest remained alone on the balcony and after half an hour interrupted a good party by shooting himself through the head."

In the second scene, the Jewish gangster Max Redlicht is locked in the Stara Boznica synagogue with Orthodox Jews. They are told to spit on the Torah scroll. "There was to be no faking – the spittle was to be visible on the calligraphy." When it came down to it, only Max Redlicht resisted. "'I've done a lot. But I won't do that.'" They shot him first, and then the rest. I think about Max Redlicht often: I ask myself, stupidly, if he was closer to God than anyone.

The urge to fictionalise is addictive, but the truth is most likely this: Redlicht knew killers when he met them.

In life, the *Schindlerjuden* were liberated by a Russian Jewish soldier. "Don't go east – that much I can tell you," he says in the novel. "But don't go west either … They don't like us anywhere." In the film, the "us" becomes "you". My fear is that Spielberg did this because these men – fiddler, gangster, liberator – were Jews with agency, however small. They do not fit his narrative. Rather, he polishes the cringing, Jewish mass – the almost dead, the pre-dead, the fated-dead – that dominates Shoah culture, denies what came before it – a great civilisation – and suggests, on what psychotherapist Warren Colman calls "an archetypal frequency", that Jews and death belong together, then and now. And he sent it out to the world.

But there is a fabrication close to the end: the one-more-life scene. Schindler collapses and weeps: he pulls out the objects he could have sold for Jews. "I could have got more. If I'd made more money. I threw away so much money. I didn't do enough." It is very capitalist, and American, and Christian: the final battle of a sinner with his conscience, among the Jews who are the instrument of his redemption. Stern tells Schindler (tells American Jewry, the viewer, the world), "You did so much." And this is absolution. He did enough, and, in watching the film – this is the insinuation – so have we.

I would like to see a Spielberg film about the gulf around the cramped margins of the list. What would that look like? Or a film of Schindler's final years, when he lived with "discouragement, loneliness, disillusion", became the dependant of the *Schindlerjuden*, and found, according to Keneally, "some of the people he had saved a little tiresomely bourgeois" because they tried to limit him to three large cognacs a night. Spielberg did make a film about Jews with rage, in 2005: *Munich*, which tells the story of Israeli vengeance after the 1972 Olympics massacre. But it was not a hit, and it was too late.

In the last scene of *Schindler's List,* Liam Neeson lays a red rose on Schindler's grave, magician to magician. Why him? To say thank you, Oskar – for the part? But – two complete Oskar Schindlers! How many lives is that? And seven Oscars! How many lives is *that*?

If Thomas Keneally writes both the Nazi rescuer and Nazi antihero, *Sophie's Choice* presents an antisemitic victim: this is the Shoah as non-Jewish tragedy. William Styron's 1979 novel is about a non-Jewish Auschwitz survivor, Sophie Zawistowska. Fiction comes from the subconscious, and it speaks to the subconscious. Sophie came to Styron in a dream: the woman who loses her children. He invented her, and I wonder if she is, at least partially, his mother Pauline, who was ill throughout his childhood, and died when he was fourteen. Styron wanted to be interesting: a tale of common maternal abandonment in Virginia may have offended his vanity. The novel may also be revenge on his wife, who came from an affluent Jewish family who initially despised Styron and did not want her to marry him: Styron was a Protestant. Sophie is Styron's creation. Yet people believe in her.

If putting your non-Jewish mother in Auschwitz is extreme, Styron had an excuse. When he was writing the novel, the established numbers of those murdered in Auschwitz were wrong. Historians believed that 2.5 million Jews died there, and 1 million non-Jews. The figures have now been amended to 1 million Jews and 100,000 non-Jews. Styron called the incorrect numbers "stupefying" enough to "signal the death of God".

"Jewish genocide became the main business of Auschwitz," he writes. But the million non-Jews – 900,000 of them fictional – were "fated to be butchered with the same genocidal ruthlessness as were the Jews, had Hitler won the war". This is untrue: the Slav nations were slave labourers, often murdered, often tortured, always used. It is a terrible fate, but the Nazis never intended to kill them all: that destiny was reserved for the Jews. Even so, Styron amends the character of the Shoah to make a non-Jew its principal victim: the rebuke to the selfish Jew, gathering all pain to himself, is implicit. He calls Auschwitz "unyielding". Rather, he is.

Among these non-Jews were "hundreds of thousands of Christians who went to their despairing deaths in the belief that their God, the Prince of Peace, was as dead as the God of Abraham and Moses". Because of this, Styron could not "accept antisemitism as the sole touchstone by which we examine the monstrous paradigm that Auschwitz has become". He did not trust the "chorus of mea culpas" from Christian theologians "rising along with the oddly self-lacerating assertion that the Holocaust came about as the result of the antisemitism embedded in Christian doctrine". The theologians were right; even so, Styron wrote *Sophie's Choice* to disprove them.

"Doomed" Sophie is beautiful, broken and remote, ideal for erotic fiction, and there is plenty of it here. All men feast on her: her mad

Jewish lover Nathan Landau (all Styron's Jews are mad, and without joy), who persecutes this non-Jew to her death; Commandant Rudolf Höss of Auschwitz (less mad, also without joy); Stingo, the narrator of the novel, a "horny Calvinist" novelist and descendant of slave owners, a man both grandiose and self-hating. This is his novel, and its theme is not the annihilation of the European Jewish nation, but his own vanity, and fear. *Sophie's Choice* is an early version of the idea, recently developed in Pankaj Mishra's essay "The Shoah after Gaza", that the "legacy" of the Shoah belongs not to Jews but to non-Jews, because they understand it better. "It is surpassingly difficult," Stingo writes, "for many Jews to see beyond the consecrated nature of the Nazis' genocidal fury." Styron is not here to divine the meaning of the Shoah: how could he when he does not want to? No, through his

> *The Jew is the downfall of the non-Jew, and the trajectory of the Shoah is reversed*

avatar Stingo he seeks "The Novel. The blessed Novel. The sacred Novel. The Almighty Novel". Stingo is jealous of Saul Bellow, and calls his *Dangling Man* "pretty thin". Is this what the book is about?

Stingo moves to a boarding house in Brooklyn, as much "the heart of Jewry" as Tel Aviv. (In the film he carries twenty-four cans of Spam into the house, so you know he is not a Jew.) There he meets Sophie and Nathan, who "lay siege to his imagination". Non-Jewish Sophie, who was in Auschwitz, is the victim of Jewish Nathan, who wasn't: "What do you know about concentration camps, Nathan Landau?" Eventually he leads her to her death: the

Jew is the downfall of the non-Jew, and the trajectory of the Shoah is reversed.

There are two types of antisemitism in this novel: the first is hostility, the second erasure. As a child, Stingo "saw how Jews seemed to acquire another self-or-being. It was out of the glare of daylight and the bustle of business, when Jews disappeared into their domestic quarantine and the seclusion of their sinister and Asiatic worship." This discomfort follows him to Brooklyn: in a restaurant "a great noise of Yiddish ... filled the dank and redolent air with unfathomable gutturals, as of many wattled old throats gargling on chicken fat". Styron is taken with Jewish speech: it is Bellow again? Stingo describes the parents of Leslie, a girl he desires and despises: "the mother pathetically overweight in the manner of Jewish mothers; the father ... able to chat only of his trade – moulded plastics – in a voice heavily inflected with the palatal gulps of his mother tongue".

Nathan is a mentally ill, abusive fantasist: the Jewish liar, and racist, of all ages. Stingo wants to school him in morality. When Nathan calls him "a cracker", Stingo replies, "Suppose I told you that somebody with a name like Landau couldn't be anything but a fat, hook-nosed, misery pawnbroker out to cheat trusting Gentiles. It would make you mad. It works both ways, these slurs."

Jews, Stingo believes, should know better: our history – really Stingo's history, the history of the antisemites – demands it.

"As a member of a race which has been unjustly persecuted
for centuries for having allegedly crucified Christ, you – yes,
you, goddammit! – should be aware of how inexcusable it is

to condemn any single people for anything! And that goes for any people," I said, "by God, even the Germans!"

This is Pankaj Mishra's argument: hey, Jews, you went to Auschwitz, were schooled in racism, and emerged more racist. (And *Dangling Man* is thin.)

It is Stingo to whom Sophie confides her experiences at Auschwitz, because her mad, racist Jewish lover cannot hear. I wonder if Nathan is mad because he has somehow got his hands on an early draft of Stingo's novel, or at least the notes. "I have thought that it might be possible to make a stab at understanding Auschwitz by trying to understand Sophie," he says. Styron then writes a monstrous libel which the novelist will call daring but incites only nausea in this Jew: "Although she was not Jewish, she had suffered as much as any Jew who had survived the same afflictions, and – as I think will be made plain – had in certain profound ways suffered more than most." Profound and *fictional* ways.

Sophie's father was a university professor. He wrote a pamphlet called "Poland's Jewish Problem: Does National Socialism Have the Answer?" That she should be sent to Auschwitz for possessing an illegal ham is, under the circumstances, quite funny. (The professor ends up a corpse in Sachsenhausen. They are an unlucky family.) Here she works in the office of Rudolf Höss, because literary novelists always give their characters a VIP pass. They cannot help it. Styron is an early and devoted chronicler of the anguish that Höss's logistical problems bring him. It's not easy being in Auschwitz in 1942! (For anyone!) This is probably the place to tell you that there is more on Höss in popular culture than there is on the entirety of Lithuanian, Russian or even Polish Jewry. He pops up in *Schindler's List*, suave this time (of course), stroking Oskar's diamonds: "I'm not saying I'm accepting them. I'm saying I'm not comfortable with them on the table." He appears in the book and film *The Zone of Interest*, and in many terrible novels. I have a note to myself saying he appeared in *Exodus* (1958) but that cannot be true. I must have dreamt it.

Höss is a character from *Springtime for Hitler*, the musical-within-a-film in Mel Brooks's *The Producers* (1967). Pitched as "a gay romp with Adolf and Eva at Berchtesgaden", the musical is written by Franz Liebkind, an ex-Nazi who talks to pigeons about how much he loves Hitler. *The Producers* is a masterpiece that exists to console Jews: it reminds us that we can laugh at Nazis and feel joy. Brooks served in the US Army in Europe in the 1940s. He went to war against Nazis in real life. William Styron went to war against Saul Bellow, and his mother. I have seen *The Producers*: there was a revival in London last year. "What a funny, silly night," one critic said as he left the theatre, having watched Mel Brooks, through his avatars Max Bialystock (luminously alive) and Leo Bloom (dead inside), split the Ashkenazi soul in two. This critic tweets against Israel daily. He did not understand what he was watching.

In what could be *Springtime*, but less self-aware, Sophie tends to Höss. She eases his migraine (I very much wanted to call this essay "Höss's Migraine: a Gay Romp through Shoah Culture"); she expresses interest in his horse. Höss is presented as a victim here, stuffed with ennui, tired of being forced to murder Jews. "Jews. Jews! Will I ever be done with Jews?" he says, when Sophie presents her antisemitic credentials. Is he speaking for the author? (It's a long novel.) Sophie isn't a real antisemite, of course. Just when it's important – when she wants Höss to let her see her son – or when Nathan is vexing her.

"Oh, it was so very Jewish of Nathan to do that – he wasn't giving me his love, he was buying me with it, like all Jews. No wonder the Jews were so hated in Europe, thinking they could get anything they wished just by paying a little money, a little Geld. Even love they think they can buy! ... Jews! God, how I hate them! ... All my childhood, all my life I really hated Jews. They deserved it, this hate. I hate them, dirty Jewish cochons!"

What Styron wants, like any tourist, is to enjoy Auschwitz. In 1974, when he was writing *Sophie's Choice*, he went there, and he wrote a column about it for the *New York Times*. Nothing would compel him to stay in Auschwitz after dark, he wrote. He was shocked that there were seasons here, because Auschwitz, like Jews themselves, was not part of this world. The article begins, in homage to *The Producers*, with the words "Springtime at Auschwitz" and goes on, wonderingly, of his hotel: "What does the guest really order for breakfast? A room with which view does one request?" He tours the "hulking and Teutonic" structures, "the mountains of human hair", "the wretched suitcases with crudely or neatly-painted names like Stein and Mendelson". He concludes that "Auschwitz must remain the one place on earth most unyielding to meaning or definition". For him, perhaps.

With one word – unyielding! – he is free, and Styron writes the Auschwitz he wants. It is, partially, an Auschwitz with sex: lesbian sex and sadomasochistic sex. Höss's housekeeper desires Sophie, giving her the underwear of dead women "so your nice bottom will stay all white and soft ... lift up your skirt a bit, darling ... no, higher!" Höss, too, desires her: "You've been flirting shamelessly with me," he tells her. "And his heart – his rampaging galloping heart! Never had she conceived that a single heart was capable of the riotous romantic thumping which moved against her like a drumbeat through the Commandant's damp shirt." Done with Nazi hearts – who would speak of them in Auschwitz? – Höss says what Styron thinks he would say, if he were a Nazi functionary contemplating ripping his uniform off: "I long to have intercourse with you."

But he doesn't. (Migraine.) Though Sophie tries. She tells Stingo later: "I surrounded Höss's boots with my arms. I pressed my cheek up against those cold leather boots. And do you know? I think maybe I even licked them with my tongue, licked those Nazi boots." Is this Styron the boy finding the most offensive thing in his heart, and writing it down?

The book's climax is the fictional, and titular, choice: Sophie must choose which of her children will live. There is not atrocity enough for Styron in Auschwitz already, so he invents Dr Jemand von Niemand ("Someone from nobody") of the SS. "And what, in the private misery of his heart, I think he most intensely lusted to do was to inflict upon Sophie, or someone like her – some tender and perishable Christian – a totally unpardonable sin."

Von Niemand was "a steadfast churchgoer and ... had always planned to enter the ministry. A mercenary father forced him into medicine." In Auschwitz, he sought "to restore his belief in God, and at the same time to affirm his human capacity for evil, by committing the most intolerable sin that he was able to conceive? Goodness could come later. But first a great sin. One whose glory lay in its subtle magnanimity – a choice." Styron's "Shoah" novel has a Christian imperative at its heart.

In 2007 Styron's daughter Alexandra wrote:

Sophie had come to him in a dream, Daddy always said. Not much older than I am now, he had woken up in Connecticut and been unable to shake the image of a woman he once knew. She'd lived above him in Flatbush, in the boarding house he immortalized as Yetta Zimmerman's Pink Palace. She was a Holocaust survivor, as evidenced by her wrist tattoo, Polish and beautiful, but more than that he didn't know.

Styron is stupefied, but the Shoah is not "stupefying". The truth – beneath Roth's "poisonous notion of being interesting or serious" – is simply this: of all the anguished, vanished Jewish mothers of Europe, Styron couldn't find one worthy of him. That was his choice. "Morning", his novel ends, "excellent and fair". I wrote beneath: *for you.*

In the BBC comedy *Extras* (2005), Kate Winslet, playing herself, says, "I don't think we really need another film about the Holocaust, do we? It's like – how many have there been? We get it. It was grim, move on." Then she concedes, "If you do a film about the Holocaust, you are guaranteed an Oscar. *Schindler's List. The Pianist.* Oscars coming out of their arse." Three years later, she won an Academy Award for playing Hanna in *The Reader.* The punchline was slow to arrive.

Hanna is the helpless victim of *The Reader* (1995), the novel by German judge Bernhard Schlink: in 2007 it was named, very precisely, Germany's fourteenth favourite book. It is a perpetrator story – the Jews are a consistent absence – and a consolation, because it tells readers that Germany butchered Jews not due to hatred, but to ignorance that is easily thwarted if only you read enough middlebrow literature. Michael Berg, fifteen, a schoolboy in post-war Germany, meets Hanna Schmitz, thirty-six, an illiterate tram conductor and murderer. They embark on an affair, which centres on bathing: she polishes him like a kettle, because Germany must be cleansed. This cleansing is relative, because this novel is filled with sex: "Her neck and shoulders, her breasts, which the petticoat veiled rather than concealed, her hips, which stretched the petticoat tight as she propped her foot on her knee and then set it on the chair, her leg, pale and naked, then shimmering in the silky stocking." But Hanna does not inhabit herself. Michael asks her about her job on the trams. "She told me all this as if it were not her life but somebody else's, someone she didn't know well and who wasn't important to her." *The Reader,* likewise, is as emotionally cauterised a novel as I have ever read: numbness is no tribute to the Jews.

Because Hanna grooms Michael, he becomes alienated from his family.

I felt as if we were sitting all together for the last time around the round table under the five-armed, five-candled brass chandelier, as if we were eating our last meal off the old plates with the green vine-leaf border, as if we would never talk to each other as a family again.

It is an imitation of other, infinitely sadder, alienations; and of Germany, which cannot go back to itself. Years later, as a law student, Michael attends Hanna's trial. In the film, his teacher is played by Bruno Ganz from *Downfall*, so, in the expanding space of the Nazi Comic Universe, Hitler is asking Michael if he is okay.

Hanna could be anyone, because she has no life of the mind. The perpetrator cannot be found. She is not here. She sews; she washes; she stares. (In the film, Winslet's beauty, and skill, makes her something else: arresting; another beautiful Nazi.) Years earlier, Michael read Tolstoy to her. The author's idea – and it is

The genocidaires were not ignorant; they were highly educated

a lawyer's book, an intellectual snob's book – is that, if Hanna had been properly educated, she would not have burned 300 Jewish women alive in a church. She remains ashamed that she cannot read; about burning 300 Jews to death she seems merely touchy.

As with Styron, the novel is based on a misapprehension. This is from Martin's Amis's 2014 novel *The Zone of Interest*: "Of the twenty-five leaders of the Einsatzgruppen in Poland and the USSR, who did some warm work I can tell you – fifteen doctorates. Now look at the Conference of State Secretaries in January. Of the fifteen attendees? Eight doctorates. At Wannsee? 'Eight doctorates,' said Professor Zulz." The genocidaires were not ignorant: that is a fantasy. They were highly educated.

Michael's generation was "Exploring the past! We tore open the windows and let in the air, the wind that finally whirled away the dust that society had permitted to settle over the horrors of the past." This approach brings him only disgust. "When I think about it now, I think that our eagerness to assimilate the horrors and our desire to make everyone else aware of them was in fact repulsive." I do not know why he thinks this, and Schlink doesn't tell me: why wouldn't Michael want to understand, and from within a novel about expiation?

Because he can't. Michael yearns to feel, but cannot. He has a "general numbness": it had "taken hold not only of the perpetrators and victims, but of all of us". In his – and presumably Schlink's – world, the Shoah has become a deadening miasma that settles on everything: an idea.

During her trial Hanna asks: "I … I mean … so what would you have done?" This was the common defence at the Nuremberg trials. Only Abby Mann's film *Judgment at Nuremberg* (1961) gives an adequate response, and it is fictional. The Nazi judge Ernst Janning (played by Burt Lancaster) says:

"I was content to sit silent during this trial. I was content to tend my roses. I was even content to let counsel try to save my name, until I realized that in order to save it, he would have to raise the spectre again. You have seen him do it – he has done it here in this courtroom ... It is not easy to tell the truth; but if there is to be any salvation for Germany, we who know our guilt must admit it ... whatever the pain and humiliation."

In *The Reader*, Hanna's question – *what would you have done?* – is left unanswered.

Hanna is presented as the object of pity here: "A life made up of advances that were actually frantic retreats and victories that were concealed defeats." Still, Michael dreams of her: the pitiful killer. (During the war, she had Jewish girls read to her, before sending them to the gas chambers. Michael dreams up a kindly rationale: she wanted them to have restful final days.) Auschwitz sex reappears:

The worst were the dreams in which a hard, imperious, cruel Hanna aroused me sexually; I woke from them full of longing and shame and rage. And full of fear about who I really was. I knew that my fantasized images were poor clichés ... But still they were very powerful. They undermined my actual memories of Hanna and merged with the images of the camps that I had in my mind.

When Hanna is later imprisoned, Michael sends her audiobooks, and she learns to read. After her death – she hangs herself the day before her release – he visits her cell and finds her books: "Primo Levi, Elie Wiesel, Tadeusz Borowski, Jean Améry – the literature of the victims, next to the autobiography of Rudolf Hess [he means Höss], Hannah Arendt's report on Eichmann in Jerusalem, and scholarly literature on the camps." Michael calls Shoah culture "part of our collective imagination". I find Schlink, in his elusions, at the edge. Surely he means collective *history*?

But Schlink can't tolerate collective history. Through Michael he says, in conclusion, "The few images derived from Allied photographs and the testimony of survivors flashed on the mind again and again, until they froze into clichés. My impressions of Struthof [a concentration camp he visits] joined my few already existing images of Auschwitz and Bergen-Belsen and froze along with them." Michael praises *Sophie's Choice* and *Schindler's List*. He needs the exonerating fictions. They console him.

At the end of the film, Michael meets a survivor of the massacre, serene in her enormous apartment, in white for purity, stripped of rage, and clearly rich: the idealised survivor in her palace. She is a repository of wisdom, even as she insists that she is not, and she tells him: "People ask all the time what I learned in the camps. But the camps weren't therapy. What do you think these places were? Universities?" (That is exactly what non-Jewish intellectuals think they were.) "We didn't go there to learn," she adds. "Go to the theatre if you want catharsis. Please. Go to literature. Don't go to the camps. Nothing comes out of the camps. Nothing." This isn't true, of course – we have Levi and Wiesel and Gradowski – but the insinuation is still: go to *The Reader* and its misapprehensions. This survivor is a critic, and she gives Schlink, her creator, a kind review.

The three most famous novels about the Shoah are by non-Jews. The first is *Schindler's Ark*; the second is *Sophie's Choice*; the last is John Boyne's *The Boy in the Striped Pyjamas*, the 2006 blockbuster of modern Shoah fiction, beloved by schoolchildren able to place themselves in Auschwitz for the duration of a short, whimsical novel. The cover blurb reads: "Lines may divide us, but hope will unite us." I don't think even Boyne believes that.

Boyne combines Keneally's and Styron's elisions – non-Jewish rescuer, non-Jewish victim – to invent a non-Jewish rescuer and victim in the form of one child:

Boyne, made famous by his Shoah novel, is immune to Jewish voices

Bruno, the son of the commandant of Auschwitz. This fiction is offensive, and dangerous, but Boyne, made famous by his Shoah novel, is immune to Jewish voices.

Boyne, a Dublin-born Catholic, has limited interest in the real Shoah. He says that he was raised to fear non-Catholics: "I knew there were Protestants in Dublin, and Methodists and Jews and Mormons, but I never laid eyes on any of them and probably would have run a mile if I had. They were going to hell, after all, or so the priests told us." To explain why he set his novel in Auschwitz, he says he wants to answer the question, "How could so many millions of people have been murdered under the eyes of the whole world without anyone knowing about it?" The question itself is wrong. His book is set in 1943–44, by which time the Shoah – though not its scale – was public knowledge. The Bund Report was released in May 1942; the Riegner telegram in November 1942; the Allied Declaration to bring war criminals to justice came in December 1942. It is true that these reports were generally disbelieved. It is also true that the novel is carefully subtitled "a fable". It does not name the Führer ("the Fury"); the death site ("Out-With") or, quite often, the victim: the Jew. It is a novel of stunning omission, but it cannot, as Boyne insists, be wrong. It is immune to criticism, like a man who has spent years in therapy and will cling to his invention or drown.

In 2020 Boyne criticised the glut of Shoah fiction that the success of his own novel incited. "Publishers & writers," he wrote, "are effectively building a genre that sells well, when in reality the subject matter ... should be treated with a little more thought & consideration." If this was from guilt it was buried deep, and I think vanity is a more likely cause. The Auschwitz Museum countered with the suggestion that Boyne's own work "should be avoided by anyone who studies or teaches the history of the Holocaust". Boyne replied that it was only "a work of fiction ... and therefore by its nature cannot contain inaccuracies, only anachronisms". He added that he "treated the subject matter with great care in my novel, although readers are of course free to feel differently". To feel differently, but not to know differently. These readers are aged eight to twelve, mostly; they are not Raul Hilberg or Lucy Dawidowicz or Yehuda Bauer.

He added: "the great joy of literature ... is that it embraces different opinions, it encourages debate, it allows us to have heated conversations with our closest friends. No one gets hurt, no one gets taken away from their homes and no one gets killed." Here, he insinuates that his Jewish critics do not understand literature as he does, and their misunderstanding is insulting to the victims he has appropriated. This confidence came late to him.

Boyne creates two nine-year-old boys, German Bruno and Jewish Shmuel. They were both born on Boyne's father's birthday, 15 April 1934, and there is a story here. He doesn't tell it. Bruno is open-hearted and good: the child of imagination. As the book opens, his family is preparing to travel to Auschwitz. Bruno doesn't want to go. His mother says: you wouldn't want your father to be lonely. She also says: we don't have a choice in this. (In truth, Hedwig Höss enjoyed living at Auschwitz.) This is Nazi humanity, and Nazi powerlessness, by emphasis. If fiction is unconscious, fable is more so.

In the house by the camp, Bruno finds his surroundings "empty and cold, as if he was in the loneliest place in the world. No one ever laughed there; there was nothing to laugh at and nothing to be happy about." Then he meets Shmuel, the most un-Jewish Jewish child in fiction, and a prisoner of Auschwitz. (As Jean-Paul Sartre wrote, "It is the anti-Semite that creates the Jew.") They realise they have the same birthday: "We're like twins," says Bruno. Shmuel agrees: "A little bit." Boyne's idea is this: their fates might have been reversed. The German child could have been the victim; perhaps the Jew could have been the perpetrator. (When I am cynical, I wonder if this is a cautionary tale about being friends with a Jew. When I am yet more cynical, I wonder if Shmuel planned the whole thing.) In any case, they are the same boy.

This might be fair, if it did not erase the history of European antisemitism: a strange thing to do for a novel set in Auschwitz. Shmuel did not arrive in Auschwitz on the turn of a card. It was not an accident, but the accumulation of something deep inside the European Christian soul: the idea of eternal, and irrevocable, Jewish guilt.

Bruno and Shmuel befriend each other and, the day before Bruno is due to leave Auschwitz, he climbs under the fence to help Shmuel find his (presumably dead) father, puts on a pair of striped pyjamas, and is gassed to death with Shmuel.

> His feet brought him up a set of steps, and as he marched on he found there was no more rain coming down anymore because they were all piling into a long room that was surprisingly warm and must have been very securely built because no rain was getting in anywhere. In fact, it felt completely airtight … "I'm sorry we didn't find your papa," said Bruno. "It's all right," said Shmuel … And then the room went very dark and some-how, despite the chaos that followed, Bruno found that he was still holding Shmuel's hand in his own and nothing in the world would have persuaded him to let it go.

The reader accepts Shmuel's fate: he is already dead. (Another Jewish inmate mirrors this: when Bruno asks how long he has lived in Auschwitz, he says, "I think I've always been here." He is one of Spielberg's fated-dead.) But we cannot accept Bruno's death, because Boyne has used his skill to make us love him. Bruno is alive to anguish, and you feel grief for him, because his fate is awry: he is not meant to be dead.

If Bruno is alive to anguish, Shmuel is alive to nothing. He feels no anger, just placidity, and the reader feels no sadness, or guilt. We are told Shmuel is bilingual – he speaks German and Polish – and his mother was a schoolteacher. Such a boy would understand what was happening to him, but he says almost nothing. Speech itself has been removed from him: he is the anti–Emanuel Ringelblum, the furious diarist of the Warsaw Ghetto. Shmuel's description of living in Auschwitz is: "It's not very nice." When Bruno causes him to be beaten, he says, "It's alright, I don't feel it anymore, I don't feel anything anymore." Bruno thinks the name Shmuel "sounds like the wind blowing". I gagged at this: dust thou art, and unto dust thou shalt return.

You feel grief for Bruno, because his fate is awry: he is not meant to be dead

The novel can be told in one scene. "I came home one day," Shmuel says, "and Mama said we couldn't live in our house anymore." "That happened to me too!" shouts Bruno. I think Shmuel and Bruno, born on the same day, are both Boyne: the one speechless and already dead; the other imaginative, and begging to live. The speechless drags the imaginative to his death. That didn't happen to John Boyne, of course: he just wrote a best-selling novel that people think is about the Shoah but is really another novel about the writer.

Boyne's own story is this: as a child, Catholic priests beat him and a Catholic teacher sexually assaulted him; later, as a gay man, Catholic doctrine induced shame in him. This novel is the howl of a child, then, in which Boyne split his soul in two, and placed it in Auschwitz, because people listen when you use the magic word. That is the novel's power, its obscenity, and the reason why he defends it, even to the Auschwitz Museum. He is defending himself. To me, Boyne reads as chronically, ragingly unseen, and this is his testimony of cruelty at the hands of the Catholic Church. Of course, now he is no longer unseen. But in disguise.

At the end of Boyne's novel our pity turns to the commandant, transformed into a loving man: in the film it is worse, as he rushes through the camp to find his child. I wonder if punishing the commandant – the father – was the point of the novel: because he did not know who his son was. He understands at last, finding Bruno's clothes by the fence, and the world mourns for the non-Jewish child of Auschwitz: the son of the perpetrator.

Boyne's book is much used in schools, and a circle closes here. With Boyne, the arc of popular Shoah fiction – the substitution of the Jew with the Christian, the replacement of the particular with the universal – is complete.

If Boyne gives us a fictional victim in Bruno, in a sequel about Bruno's sister Gretel, *All the Broken Places* (2022), he gives us a fictional penitent. It is narrated by Gretel at the end of her life. Gretel, who has the disinterested voice of a mature novelist, is contrite:

so much so that, when she learns that the owner of the flat downstairs is beating his child, she cuts his throat with a box-cutter. "I did it for an innocent nine-year-old boy. To save him." She doesn't say if she means Bruno or Shmuel. It does not matter, though, because, as we know from the first book, they are the same person: "It was almost (Shmuel thought) as if they were all exactly the same really." At the end of the novel, after Gretel has demonstrated contrition in multiple scenarios, and even had a child by a Jew, she says: "The words are too simple, I know, and will be of little comfort to anyone, but I mean them. I am so sorry."

The real Höss children are not penitent, or even shocked. This is fiction and, as Cynthia Ozick says, the rights of fiction are not the rights of history. In 2024, two of Höss's five children – Hans-Jürgen and Brigitte (Puppi) appeared in the documentary *The Commandant's Shadow*. Here is their testimony.

Hans-Jürgen: "I had a really lovely and idyllic childhood in Auschwitz. We paddled on the river with my father or played with the dogs in the garden. We had everything."

"I never found out what was really going on there when I was a child," he says. "My father never told us anything about his work, nothing at all." In a family photograph from that time Hans-Jürgen looks haunted: children know things without knowing that they know them. "I think he [their father] did paperwork," he says, "got things done. That was it. I don't think he dealt with anything personally. Had something been not quite right and there had been smoke, I would have seen it, I would have known. It would never have occurred to me that they were burning people."

On screen he meets up with Puppi. She looks like an ancient child. "We had a beautiful mother and father," Puppi says. "He [their father] was a good person. He got into it, and he couldn't get out of it. Mummy went along with everything. She shielded us from everything and made everything lovely for us. Mummy went through a lot. And she was always kind. I never saw anything bad in Auschwitz. Everything was always beautiful. Then the war ended and everything fell to pieces. In life not everything goes as you want." She is not Gretel, then.

"I said I will never be angry with my dad," she continues. "He must have been a very strong person to live like this and do what he had to do. And look at all the people who said they died in the camp but [were] all the survivors. Why didn't they die? They are still living, they get money from Germany, the Jewish people, you know." She ends: "So whatever you want to believe you do."

And that is Bruno and Gretel, or as close as we will get to them. They did not have the narrative arc – for one death, for the other redemption – that Boyne wrote for them, which he needs so badly and defends so doggedly, even to the point of telling the Auschwitz Museum that he is right, and they are wrong. Bruno and Shmuel, one loving, one speechless, both dead, both Boyne. I would tell him, since he is an adult: there's a difference between a real child who is innocent – as Hans-Jürgen was – and a fictional child invented to be innocent. The first has no cynicism; the second is all cynicism.

To Boyne, it doesn't matter. He remains proud of *The Boy in the Striped Pyjamas* for the very reason he should feel ashamed: "It has become, for a generation of young people around the world, their first introduction to a study of the Holocaust." He has always, he says, "made sure to impress on young readers the fact that this is a work of fiction – a fable – and to list the titles I would recommend they read next". Is it petty to say that, in my Kindle edition, no such list of recommended titles exists – beyond a link to more works by John Boyne?

Jonathan Littell is a French-American writer of Russian-Jewish descent. His debut novel, *The Kindly Ones* (2006), is over 900 pages long and learned: it was, when published, a sensation among intellectuals. It is the memoir of a fictional SS officer at "the heart of the slaughterhouse", Maximilien Aue. It is a literary novel, but reads like Hannibal Lecter meets the SS; or Zelig of the Nazi Comic Universe. Aue flies across Europe – from Babi-Yar to Stalingrad to Auschwitz to Berlin – with a copy of Flaubert's *Sentimental Education* in his luggage. His other book is *Jewish Ritual Murder: A Historical Investigation*, by Hellmut Schramm: an account of Jewish murders of children in history. He meets Adolf Hitler, and Heinrich Himmler, and Adolf Eichmann. He drowns in blood, and lives without regret.

Aue "never asked to become a murderer". He would have liked to be a novelist. He calls his memoir "a real morality play. And also, this concerns you: you'll see that this concerns you." He does "not regret anything: I did my work, that's all." There is no contrition here. Just constipation. Aue is dogged by it and has written a memoir that the surviving SS men of Odessa – their post-war trade union – would love.

Aue the monster misses Death. Even now he says, after the war, "my head begins to rage, with the dull roar of a crematorium. Standing at a bar with my glass of Cognac," he dreams of atrocity, because he is "curious". About the killing, he wants to know "what effect all this would have on me". He is speaking for the reader who would place himself in Auschwitz to see how it feels: this is *The Boy in the Striped Pyjamas* for adults.

He is echoing what Primo Levi, a chemist, wrote in *If This Is a Man*:

> We are in fact convinced that no human experience is without meaning or unworthy of analysis, and that fundamental values, even if they are not positive, can be deduced from this particular world which we are describing. We would also like to consider that the Lager [Auschwitz] was pre-eminently a gigantic biological and social experiment.

Aue (or perhaps Littell) is Primo Levi without love; after what he went through, Levi had less cause to feel love, but he had more of it.

Levi's response to his reality was, in fact, the opposite of Littell's fiction. Levi, a real man, believed in civilisation, even in Auschwitz. Aue, a fiction, does not.

> We do not believe in the most obvious and facile deduction: that man is fundamentally brutal, egoistic and stupid in his conduct once every civilized institution is taken away, and that

the Häftling [prisoner] is consequently nothing but a man without inhibitions. We believe, rather, that the only conclusion to be drawn is that in the face of driving necessity and physical disabilities many social habits and instincts are reduced to silence.

Aue does not love Jews. He thinks we are like Nazis, as modern antisemites do.

The Jews too had this strong feeling of community, of Volk: they mourned their dead, buried them if they could and said Kaddish; but as long as one single Jew remained alive, Israel lived. That, no doubt, was the reason they were our privileged enemies, they resembled us too much.

At one point he hallucinates that Adolf Hitler is a rabbi:

I opened my eyes wide: on his head and shoulders, over his simple feldgrau uniform, I seemed to see a large blue-and-white striped rabbi's shawl. The Führer had started speaking right away in his rapid, monotone voice. I examined the glass roof: Could it be a play of the light? I could clearly see his cap; but underneath it, I thought I made out long side curls, unrolling along his temples down over his lapel, and on his forehead, the tefillin, the little leather box containing verses of the Torah.

"Now of course the war is over," Aue writes. "And we've learned our lesson, it won't happen again. But are you quite sure we've learned our lesson? Are you certain it won't happen again? Are you even certain the war is over?" This is decadence: of course the war is over, if the war is real.

I will quote Levi again, specifically his response to Liliana Cavani, who made *The Night Porter* (1974), one of many Jewsploitation films – including *Marathon Man* and *The Boys From Brazil* – that were popular in the 1970s. *The Night Porter* is about the sadomasochistic relationship between an SS officer (played by Dirk Bogarde) and a former prisoner (Charlotte Rampling). On the film's release, Cavani expressed a similar decadence. She said, "We are all victims or murderers, and we accept these roles voluntarily."

Levi replied: "I do not know, and it does not much interest me to know, whether in my depths there lurks a murderer, but I do know that I was a guiltless victim and I was not a murderer."

Höss is in *The Kindly Ones*, with an awful inevitability: if he wasn't I might have missed him. He is "hardworking, stubborn, and of limited abilities, without any whims or imagination, but with just, in his movements and conversation, a little of the virility, already diluted by time, left by a youth rich in Freikorps brawls and cavalry charges". Höss complains, of course. "Ever since the Reichsführer decided to allocate Auschwitz for the destruction of the Jews, we've had nothing but problems. The oven of Crematorium III cracked two weeks after it was put into service."

Mrs Höss, meanwhile, wears stolen knickers: her underwear defines her. (Even Nazis can be victims of misogyny.)

[Aue] looked at her and thought about her cunt, under her dress, nesting in the lace panties of a pretty young Jewish girl gassed by her husband. The Jewess had long ago been burned along with her own cunt and had gone up in smoke to join the clouds; her expensive panties, which she might have put on especially for her deportation, now adorned and protected the cunt of Hedwig Hoss.

Aue is less interested in Jews than in knickers: he can barely see Jews. Rather, he talks about Nazi sexual dysfunction, which is rampant, and, after the pleas of Höss's son (Hans-Jurgen?), follows some ants into a crematorium. He tells the child: "They found something to eat." He revels in obscenity, and the reader must too: "the name, now well known, of *Endlösung*: the 'Final Solution'. But what a beautiful word!" And, writing after the foundation of Israel, he says, "It's the Jews who are becoming warriors again, who are becoming cruel, who also are becoming killers. I find that very beautiful."

This is a riveting though immoral novel, because it embodies an obsession with perpetrators, and because it is fun to read: Shoah fiction should not be fun to read. For instance, towards the end Aue meets Hitler. "So, I leaned forward and bit into his bulbous nose, drawing blood. I just couldn't restrain myself." That is the novel in a scene: a bite on the nose from a man with a thesaurus – for what, who can say? Aue flees to the final scene in the Berlin Zoo. "In the lane a little elephant came trotting toward me, followed by three chimpanzees and an ocelot. I remained alone with the dying hippopotamus, a few ostriches, and the corpses."

When you read immoral Shoah culture, moral culture rebukes you. The nihilism, the bloody fun, of *The Kindly Ones* made me think of a story in Claude Lanzmann's memoir *The Patagonian Hare*. In Poland he found Henryk Gawkowski, the train driver who delivered the Jews to Treblinka as a young man, numbed by triple vodka rations, at his home.

Though I apologized for showing up so late, he seemed so unsurprised by my urgency that it was as though he shared it. He had neither forgotten nor recovered from the horrifying past in which he had played a role, and he found it entirely just that he should have to answer any demands made on him at any hour. In fact, I was the first person ever to question him; I had arrived in the night like a ghost, no one before me having troubled to hear what he had to say.

When I said, "When you pulled the wagons up to the ramp" he stopped me dead. "No, no, that's not how it happened, I didn't pull them, I pushed them," and he balled his fist and made a pushing gesture. I was devastated by this detail, floored by this truth, by which I mean that this trivial confirmation told me more, helped me more to imagine, to understand than any pompous reflection on evil doomed to reflect only on itself.

While reading *The Kindly Ones*, the critic Rob Doyle took psilocybin. "As the effects took hold," he wrote in *Unherd*, "I felt myself being submerged in the hellish, quicksand imagery and suffocating nihilism of Littell's novel. The universe was evil – life itself was an infinite gas chamber." He is responding to Aue's dream, in the novel, of a self-replicating death camp: "When I woke up," Aue says, "it seemed obvious to me that these serene dreams, void of all anguish, represented the camp, but a perfect camp, having reached an impossible point of stasis, without violence, self-regulated, functioning perfectly and also perfectly useless since, despite all this movement, it produced nothing." The effect fades, of course; the fairyland gas chamber ebbs away, and Doyle finds himself alive, and with a review to write. Doyle notes, "I finished the novel in sunlight."

I asked him: why do people visit Auschwitz? He replied, "They enjoy it"

When you gain access to the inner lives of Nazis, you get Höss's prison memoirs, or Franz Stangl of Treblinka's stunned testimony to Gitta Sereny in *Into That Darkness: An Examination of Conscience.* Or you get Josef Oberhauser of the SS, a man who looked pleasingly like the cinema villain Hugo Weaving, hiding from Claude Lanzmann in a restaurant kitchen in *Shoah*, while his colleague – who I happily imagine knew he'd butchered Jews – laughed at his discomfort. (It is the only comic scene in *Shoah*.) What you don't get is Aue. No Aue exists, or could exist, and he casts no light beyond the joy some take in Jewish murder. *The Kindly Ones* is pleasure in atrocity: it has been flung out of *Cabaret*, which lingers over Shoah fiction like a gaudy cloud. Still, it won two major literary prizes in France, as well as the *Literary Review* Bad Sex in Fiction Award in Britain, for this: "I came suddenly, a jolt that emptied my head like a spoon scraping the inside of a soft-boiled egg."

In all, the novel reminded me of a British tour guide I met in Cracow, who I think moved to Poland to be antisemitic. After he told me the Polish Jews had controlled the city before the war, I asked him: why do people visit Auschwitz? He replied, and I think he is right, "They enjoy it."

Aue ends up in France, running a lace factory, like P.G. Wodehouse's fascist leader Roderick Spode.

Martin Amis wrote two novels about the Shoah: *Time's Arrow: Or the Nature of the Offence* (1991) and *The Zone of Interest*, one element of which – the perpetrator's story – became an Academy Award–winning film in 2023, the year that Amis died. For me, Amis is the best of the Shoah novelists, for the simple reason that he obviously cared. He proves that it is possible to write non-exploitative Shoah fiction, if you take the trouble to know Jewish people. His rivals in the field – Boyne and Styron particularly – write about Jews as if they have never met one.

Time's Arrow is a dream: it could be a weighty episode of *Dr Who*. There are many fantasies in Shoah culture, from *The Painted Bird* (1965), to *The Plot Against America* (2004) to *Inglourious Basterds* (2009) but this, for me, is the most beautiful. Though it is tender – Amis cares about what happened to the Jews, he had a Jewish wife and children, which I think is why he returned to the subject – the novel is an unfulfilled wish, or a prayer. Amis was too honest to ask for redemption: not for him the fake contrition of a Nazi judge, however literate (*Judgment at Nuremberg*) or the fake vengeance of Jewish soldiers, however soothing (*Inglourious Basterds*). Amis was made so incredulous by the Shoah, he offers magic as the only antidote – this is wry from a humanist – because he knows it will fail. It is testimony to his powerlessness, and his longing. No serious person, Amis wrote, quoting W.G. Sebald, thinks about anything but the Shoah. He does not come with a sack to carry it off and make it his own. He approaches on his knees.

Time's Arrow is the story of a Nazi doctor: Dr Tod Friendly. At the beginning of the novel – which is at the end of his life – he is living in America pondering the inadequacy of civilisation: "Greta Garbo, I read, has been reborn as a cat. All this stuff about twins. A Nordic superrace will shortly descend from the cosmic iceclouds; they will rule the earth for a thousand years. All this stuff about Atlantis." But Amis performs a spell to reverse time and send Friendly back to the Shoah. The doctor's "dreams are full of figures who scatter in the wind like leaves, full of souls who form constellations like the stars I hate to see".

> I thought (I was sure) that our transgression would be some kind of departure. I thought it would be extraterritorial, out of society, forming its own new universe. And yet it turns out to be the same old stuff only worse, more, again, further. I mean, where is the limit? Show me the ultimate intensifiers of sin. What can you categorically not do to someone else's body? I've got to get over it. I keep expecting the world to make sense. It doesn't. It won't. Ever.

Amis also writes about a perpetrator: but what is different here? Simply put, it is tenderness. Unlike Styron and Boyne, who work hard to conceal the offence, Amis knows its gravity; he kicks the Nazis not because he wants to examine his own morality within the boundaries of Auschwitz, or write "the blessed novel", which his own life is too narrow to furnish, but because he hates them. He does not, as Styron and Boyne do, amend the record in service of himself. Rather, he writes poetry as tribute and spell to bring the Jews back. The thing I love most about Amis's writing is that he does not mind failing. Except here.

It is not easy to read *Time's Arrow*: always, when dealing with Shoah fiction, a sign of quality. "Auschwitz lay around me, miles and miles of it, like a somersaulted Vatican. Our preternatural purpose? To dream a race. To make a people from the weather. From thunder and from lightning. With gas, with electricity, with shit, with fire."

The Jews are reconstituted – Boyne and Styron do not seem morally conscious they existed, or have gone – "looking for the souls of their mothers and their fathers, their women and their children, gathering in the heavens – awaiting human form, and union ... The sky above the Vistula is full of stars. I can see them now. They no longer hurt my eyes."

Sometimes he offers analysis through poetry: "It is a commonplace to say that the triumph of Auschwitz was essentially organizational: we found the sacred fire that hides in the human heart – and built an autobahn that went there."

Even the reconstitution is imperfect.

The Jews were made to wait too long in summer meadows, under racing skies, where families were often united by procedures that involved too much suspense, with children running this way and that and stopping still with their hands raised like claws, searching, and babies on the ground every few yards in shawls, crying, with no parents readily available, for much too long …

Then Amis wrote a second book. Because the spell failed. They did not come back.

I know that, before he wrote *The Zone of Interest*, Martin Amis read Rudolf Höss's prison diary: a book that William Styron recommended to rabbis in *Sophie's Choice*. Because if Jews can learn morality from William Styron, why not also learn it from Höss, their murderer?

Höss was a good Nazi: compliant. When he was told to murder Jews he did. When he was told to repent, he did. He wrote a prison diary before he was hanged in 1947 and I think it is, to paraphrase Max Bialystock, the worst book ever written; either that or his translator hated him. This is Hans-Jürgen and Puppi's father. He seems barely real.

Höss is a lonely child – who knew? He doesn't really like people – who knew? He lets his horse Hans sleep in his bedroom. He calls his fellow SS officers of Dachau "Old Dachauites", as if it were an English public school. (Do they have a tie and cricket team?) At Dachau he is in charge of a gay Romanian prince who wanks himself to death. (I cannot face asking the historian at Yad Vashem if this is true.) But Dachau is a "dead-end job". And his task at Auschwitz is

not an easy one. Within a few months, I might even say during the first weeks, I became bitterly aware that all good will and all the best intentions were doomed to be dashed to pieces against the human inadequacy and sheer stupidity of most of the officers and men posted to me. Whether it was a question of bread or meat or potatoes, it was I who had to go and find them. Yes, I even had to visit the farms in order to collect straw.

He hates Auschwitz: "My only desire then was to run away and be alone and never see anyone again." The Jews are "mainly persecuted by members of their own race, their foremen or room seniors. I must emphasize here that I have never personally hated the Jews." Also, he has always respected women. The Auschwitz dog squad is useless: "Either they played games with their dogs, or found an easy hideout and went to sleep, their dogs waking them up on the approach of an 'enemy', or else passed the time in pleasant conversation with the female supervisors or the prisoners." The Auschwitz dogs are similarly useless:

It was also proposed that dogs should replace the guards in the watchtowers. They were to be allowed to run loose between the double wire fencing that encircled the camp or the permanent places of work, each dog guarding a certain sector, and would give warning of the approach of a prisoner, thus preventing a break through the wire. This, too, came to nothing. The dogs either found a spot in which to go to sleep, or they let themselves be tricked.

Tricked? Do the Elders of Zion have a Dog Section? "Neither mechanical devices nor animals can replace human intelligence." Nevertheless, in hindsight:

I also see now that the extermination of the Jews was fundamentally wrong. Precisely because of these mass exterminations, Germany has drawn upon herself the hatred of the entire world. It in no way served the cause of anti-Semitism, but on the contrary brought the Jews far closer to their ultimate objective.

His postscript? He does not know how many people he killed. Logistics!

When he read this, I know Amis thought – because I can hear him thinking it – is this it? Is this the mind that sent European Jewry to its end? No, Rudolf, says Amis, this will not do. I will do it for you. I will do it better. If the Poles hanged your body, I will hang your soul. I will make you worthy of your crimes. And so, he rewrote it as Höss might have written it if he had trusted the people he was writing for (if they were not about to kill him): and if he could write. He writes it in the style of Adrian Mole – it is definitely, and lovingly, *Springtime for Hitler* – but offers, too, a caution that the magic will not work. Because it never does. The epigraph is from *Macbeth*:

"Sweltered venom sleeping got, Boil thou first i' the charmed pot."
Amis came to the Shoah "incredulous". He remained so.

The Zone of Interest has three narrators: the first is Angelus
Thomsen, an SS officer, and nephew to Martin Bormann, Hitler's
private secretary. He is the un-stupid, self-aware Nazi. He likes
women: "I had hoiked up and unfurled many a three-ply dirndl,
I had eased off many a pair of furry bloomers, I had tossed over
my shoulder many a hobnailed clog." He calls Hitler's support-
ers "assorted tub-thumpers and layabouts, cranks and freebooters,
embittered militiamen, power-mad ploughboys, disillusioned sem-
inary students, and ruined storekeepers" who cannot win a war.
He understands that their "ten-year Walpurgisnacht is coming
to an end".

Throughout the novel, he is charged by Bormann to find out if
the "cosmic-ice theory" is true. This is an obscure, entirely true cor-
ner of Nazism: some Nazis thought they might be descended from
space aliens. As Thomsen tells his uncle, the theory

> "holds that the earth was created when a frozen comet the
> size of Jupiter collided with the sun. During the trillennia
> of winter that followed, the first Aryans were cautiously
> moulded and formed. Thus, Onkel, only the inferior races
> are descended from the great apes. The Nordic peoples were
> cryogenically preserved from the dawn of terrestrial time –
> on the lost continent of Atlantis."
>
> "… Lost how?"
>
> "Submerged, Onkel."

"And that's it?"

"Pretty much."

The residual glamour – the beautiful suits! – of Nazism dissolves in satire.

The second narrator is Paul Doll, who is really Rudolf Höss, and this is his creed: "For I am a normal man with normal needs. I am completely normal. This is what nobody seems to understand. Paul Doll is completely normal." He is self-pitying – "It seems, these days, these nights, that whenever I go to the ramp something dreadful happens – I mean to me personally" – and is dogged by problems, including the health of his children's pony: "First mange, then blister-beetle poisoning. And what's his latest stunt? Glanders." But even Doll has moments of clarity: "Why did the lunatics, and only the lunatics, seem to like it here?" His colleague tells him: "They'll fight to the last bullet [at Stalingrad]". Doll replies: "Do they have any bullets?" The clarity doesn't last. He tells his (imprisoned) girlfriend: "And you're a subhuman. Technically I mean." At his nadir he tries to murder a tortoise, falls over, and his trousers fall down.

Doll has a talent for cliché (a tabloid murderer, if you will): Amis, ever self-aware, called his collection of literary criticism *The War Against Cliché*. Amis's raging intellectual snobbery is here. Of a popular Nazi operetta Doll recalls numbly: "*The frost's destroyed the tubers, Otto*, was one of its lines, and *Get your toffee nose out of that book, can't you?* was another." But sometimes even Amis's words fail him, and this is his ultimate tribute to the Jews. Unfiltered words. "Doll's nothing," he writes. "He's shit. He's just a cunt." I see Amis writing it late at night, and re-reading in the morning. No, I imagine him thinking, leave it in. It's true.

The third narrator is Szmul Zacharias, a Jewish *Sonderkommando*. "We are of the *Sonderkommando*, the SK, the Special Squad, and we are the saddest men in the Lager," Szmul says. "We are in fact the saddest men in the history of the world. And of all these very sad men I am the saddest." Szmul is the essential character in *The Zone of Interest*, and his part is the smallest. I have laughed at Nazis before, from Charlie Chaplin's *The Great Dictator* to Quentin Tarantino's *Inglourious Basterds* (echoing Amis: "He's shit. He's just a cunt." Essentially, that's the whole film). I have never fully understood the *Sonderkommando*, even though I have read their testimony. They leave things unsaid. I do not know how they did it. Amis believes you can touch the Shoah if you are worthy; that Theodor Adorno's line, which he retracted – "To write a poem after Auschwitz is barbaric" – was not an edict but a warning. "Only a victim has the right to say there's no coming back from it," Amis wrote. "And they hardly ever do. They're desperate to restart their lives."

Here is Szmul: "I feel we are dealing with propositions and alternatives that have never been discussed before, have never needed to be discussed before. I feel that if you knew every day, every hour, every minute of human history, you would find no exemplum, no model, no precedent."

"There persist," he explains,

three reasons, or excuses, for going on living: first, to bear witness, and, second, to exact mortal vengeance. Third, and most crucially, we save a life (or prolong a life) at the rate of one per transport. Sometimes none, sometimes two – an average of one. And 0.01 per cent is not 0.00.

He is writing his own testimony:

Although I live in the present, and do so with pathological fixity, I remember everything that has happened to me since I came to the Lager. Everything. To remember an hour would take an hour. To remember a month would take a month. I cannot forget because I cannot forget. And now at the last all these memories will have to be dispersed. There is only one possible outcome, and it is the outcome I want. With this I prove that my life is mine, and mine alone. On my way over there I will inhume everything I've written, in the Thermos flask beneath the gooseberry bush. And, by reason of that, not all of me will die.

He does die, of course: he predicts it.

If it should happen that I go to the gas, I will weave among them. I will weave among them, saying, to the old man in the astrakhan coat, "Stand as close to the meshed shaft as you can, sir." Saying, to the boy in the sailor suit, "Breathe deeply, my child."

Szmul is Zalmen Gradowski, the Polish Jew who buried his testimony in the ash at Auschwitz in a bottle; and Ernie Levy of André

Schwarz-Bart's *The Last of the Just*, holding the children in his arms; and Elie Wiesel, losing his mother in eight words ("Men to the left! Women to the right!"). He knows words can do much, and still: "I need something more than words."

Szmul meets a boy he knew before, and I quote their interaction in full, because it is the shattered heart of *The Zone of Interest*.

He is club-footed – and his surgical boot will have been left in the stack on the platform, along with all the other trusses and braces and prostheses. "Witold?" I say.

"Witold." He looks up at me, and after a moment of emptiness his face flares with gratitude and relief. "Mr Zachariasz! Where's Chaim? I went looking for him."

"Went looking for him where?"

"At the bakery. It's shut. It's boarded up. I asked next door and they said Chaim went ages ago. With you and Schol."

"And his mother? His mother? Pani Zachariasz?"

"They said she went too."

"On a transport?"

"No. Walking. Her brother took her. Mr Zachariasz, I got arrested! At the station. For vagrancy. Pawiak Prison! We thought they were going to shoot us but they changed their minds. Is Chaim here?"

"Yes, he's here," I say. "Witold, come with me. Come on. Come." It is spring in the birch wood. The silver bark is peeling; the brisk wind frees droplets of moisture from the papery leaves.

Chaim is dead: he is one of the silent boys of Chełmno, murdered in the snow. Szmul tells Witold:

"Yes, Chaim's here. With his brother. They're working in the home farm. In the fields. With any luck you'll get the same job. They're big boys now. They've grown."

"What about my boot? I'll be needing my boot for the fields."

"All the luggage will be waiting at the guest house." A sound makes me look up: Doll's staff car, its flabby bald tyres slithering furiously in the mud. I gesture to Krebbs. "You'll get cheese sandwiches straight away, and then there'll be a hot meal later on. I'll have Chaim come and find you."

"Oh, that'd be good." And those are his last words.

Now he falls as if in a swoon. Krebbs steps back. It takes Witold less than a minute to die. About twenty seconds pass, and he is gone. There are fewer things to say goodbye to, there is less life, less love (perhaps), and less memory needing to be scattered.

At the beginning of *The Zone of Interest*, Amis imagines a magic mirror made by a wizard for a king. "This mirror didn't show you your reflection. It showed you your soul – it showed you who you really were." If you could stare into it for one minute, you were promised treasure. "And no one could. Under National Socialism you looked in the mirror and saw your soul. You found yourself out. Who somebody really was. That was the zone of interest."

Szmul could not have faced the mirror. Yet, in him, we are shown a complete, heroic Jew amid the Auschwitz fictions. Despite this, he is not in Jonathan Glazer's 2024 film adaptation. Glazer uses only one of Amis's perspectives: Doll's, though he calls him Höss. ("I am completely normal.") It is Höss's film, and it is a migraine. It echoes *A Real Pain*, Jesse Eisenberg's 2024 film about two American-Jewish boys, the grandsons of a survivor, visiting Poland and sinking to anguish. It has a similar fragility, and speechlessness, which speaks to Jewish grief (Glazer, like Eisenberg, is Jewish). How can we look?

By not looking, is Glazer's answer: this is a safe film, a bourgeois film, above all a pretty film. It is *Springtime for Hitler: The Minor Functionaries*. Aktion! Seed catalogues! Ice swastikas! Höss has a horse's haircut. (He stole it from Hans.) I wonder if it shares something with *The Sopranos*: it's about a man turning forty. Who happens to be a mob boss. (Who happens to be commandant of Auschwitz.)

Glazer's camera creeps around the House of Höss; it half looks. This is less a film than an aesthetic, and the aesthetic is overwhelming. The Auschwitz Flower Show: behold the dahlias! The Auschwitz Fashion Show: Helga Höss in front of a mirror, in a Jew's coat and a Jew's lipstick. (Auschwitz shows you who you are? Not she.) Rudolf in disco white; in SS-branded swimming trunks. Do they get skis? They say things like: "Did you know that storks fly as far as Africa?" and "Will you take me to that spa in Italy again? [Remember] that man who played the accordion to cows?" If it is about anything, it is about a marriage.

Towards the end of the film, Höss is travelling, and he telephones his wife. They have this conversation.

Höss: "I wasn't really paying attention [at the theatre]. I was too busy wondering how I would gas everyone in the room."

Helga: "It's the middle of the night."

Höss: "I was just excited to tell you the name."

(It was Operation Höss: the gassing of Hungarian Jews.)

The Jews here are not Spielberg's cringing mass. They are diminished yet further: they are a sound over the wall. They are an idea. I argue with people about *The Zone of Interest*. I say I am tired of a Shoah without Jews. I am tired of fictional perpetrators: of their headaches, and their dahlias and their issues with childcare. They tell me: it *is* about Jews. Jews unseen, and unnamed, but still beloved by those who see them despite their material absence. Jews behind the wall.

Did we not understand, until we watched this film, that the perpetrators are real people?

There are, in fact, more cleaners in Glazer's film than there are Jews, and at the end they clean a gas chamber. Did we not understand, until we watched this film – this film that dares not look, and calls it looking – that the perpetrators are real people? Is this the antidote to the fictions?

I prefer Woody Allen's version of *The Zone of Interest*. It is a scene from *Hannah and Her Sisters* (1986), and it is 1 minute, 23 seconds long. Lee (Barbara Hershey) returns home to her lover, Frederick (Max von Sydow), an artist.

Frederick: You missed a very dull TV show about Auschwitz. More gruesome film clips, and more puzzled intellectuals declaring their mystification over the systematic murder of millions. The reason why they [scholars] can never answer the question, "how could it possibly happen?" is that it's the wrong question. Given what people are, the question is: why doesn't it happen more often? Of course it does, in subtler forms.

Lee [speaking for the world]: I have a little headache from this weather.

Frederick: It's been ages since I sat in front of the TV just changing channels to find something. You see the whole culture. Nazis, deodorant salesmen, wrestlers, beauty contest, the talk show. Can you imagine the level of a mind that watches wrestling? But the worst are the fundamentalist preachers. Third-rate conmen telling the poor suckers that watch them that they speak for Jesus. And to please send in money. Money, money, money. If Jesus came back and saw what's going on in his name, he'd never stop throwing up.

Lee [speaking for the world]: Oh God, Frederick, could you please lighten up?

I'm glad Frederick mentioned Jesus, who could identify what has happened to Shoah culture. Something similar happened to him.

This is the Age of Stupid, and Shoah fiction has got better, and worse: better because it has lost its pseudo-sophistication and is now pulp fiction, and worse for the same reason. The de-Judaisation is complete – Boyne completed it when he gassed little Bruno Höss – and the contemporary novels treat Auschwitz as a painted curtain, or Oz. Little Dorothy could always go home, she just didn't know it.

John Donoghue is a British musician and mental health specialist. His 2015 novel, *The Death's Head Chess Club*, is a thriller (cosy Nazi?) set in what the novelist thinks is Auschwitz, but which no one with any taste, or learning, would recognise as such. It has a handsome SS officer (when are they not?): "Meissner is tall, even for a German. His hair is dark, but his eyes are a shimmering blue, disconcertingly so." Meissner's biggest headache is SS morale: more Nazis with headaches.

Meissner's Jewish antagonist, a chess player, "used to have a name, but that was in another life, a life that made sense beyond the daily struggle merely to survive". In time, his name arrives. "His name was Emil Clément, and he was a watchmaker. Now he is simply Häftling5 number 163291."

The book follows dual narratives: Amsterdam in 1962, and Auschwitz in 1944. In Amsterdam, Emil is haunted by the Shoah: "after nearly twenty years, still it followed him everywhere". He exists only for his hatred for the Germans, "nurtured, as a parent would a child, until it was almost the only thing that gave him any meaning. Hatred and chess: was that the sum total of his existence? *What kind of a life is that?*"

He meets people who tell him: "Hasn't anyone told you – the war is over. It is time to move on." How can the Jew, if even the novelist can't?

In Auschwitz, the SS decide to form a chess club for morale.

Meissner is doubtful: "he had been thinking more along the lines of a choir." But chess it is. "The *SS-Totenkopfverbände* Chess Championship could become an annual event, hosted by K-Z Auschwitz. Would that not more than fulfil the directive to boost morale?"

Emil is skilled at chess for mystical reasons: "My system is based on the Kabbalah." He is made to play chess with Nazis, and he plays for Jewish lives. (This echoes *Hunters*, a 2020 TV show in which Nazis played human chess with Jews as pieces. The weary Auschwitz Museum objected again.)

Back in Amsterdam, Emil is stalked by – why not? – a bishop. It is former SS-Chessführer Meissner, returned from penal servitude and a spell in a leper colony, now dying of leukaemia. He is, he insists, a good man: "I never set foot on the unloading ramp and took no part in any of the *Selektionen*." (Should I tell him? *Neither did Adolf Hitler*.) "Not one prisoner in Auschwitz died because of me."

Meissner is having a spiritual crisis. "I know that I have God's forgiveness, but that is not enough for me. What I hope is that I can help you to understand that the power of forgiveness will bring healing for you – not me, not anyone else." Emil, you understand, has failed the test of Auschwitz: he cannot forgive. (His wife and sons are dead.) "I still believe," Meissner adds, "that God has a definite purpose for my life. Watchmaker, that purpose is you." He uses Emil's Auschwitz name. The class system is intact.

"You say I must forgive," says Emil, "but if it's not you I have to forgive, then who?" Meissner replies, "You must learn to forgive yourself." Here, Auschwitz is a collaborative enterprise between Jew and non-Jew, and they will absolve themselves together.

Emil has flashbacks to Auschwitz, where Meissner gave him a handkerchief. "You would not have known how beautiful it was to feel again clean, white linen between my fingers. I was reluctant to soil its purity by using it to wipe away the blood." I think of a line from *The Tall Guy*, in which a beleaguered character says: "I've never had a toothpick of my own before."

There is truer writing from Zalmen Gradowski, the *Sonderkommando* who buried his testimony in the ashes at Auschwitz. He is on an "island of the dead" where eternity, "has drawn its border". Each day he drowns "in a sea, a sea of blood". He wrote a report in Yiddish about the gassing of 5000 Czech Jews on Purim in 1944. The Jews leave the trucks "without resistance – and fall fainting like mown grass into our arms. And before going down into the deep bunker, before they take the first step to the grave, they give one last look at the sky and moon – and a deep sigh escapes instinctively from both our hearts together."

Here, Auschwitz is a collaborative enterprise between Jew and non-Jew

Now naked,

many tear themselves away and fall wildly screaming and crying on those who have just arrived – these are children who have caught sight of their mothers, who kiss them, hug them, rejoice that they are here together again. For a child is glad that a mother, a mother's heart, will go with her to death.

Soon, he tells us,

from the pearly mouth – teeth and flesh together will be ripped out and much blood will spill. From that chiseled nose – two streams will run, red, yellow or white. And that face, all pink and white – will turn red, blue or black from the gas. The eyes will be so red with blood that you will not recognize that it's the same woman who stands here now. And from that head with locks of wavy hair, two cold hands will cut off the hair and from the ears and hands remove the rings and earrings … They will drag her, this lovely young blossom, over the cold, filthy cement floor. And the body will sweep with it all the dirt it finds along the way.

Gradowski now stands "near a group of women – ten or fifteen in number – and all of them, their bodies and their lives, will soon be in a single wheelbarrow". Gradowski died in the *Sonderkommando* uprising of 7 October 1944. His first manuscript was dug up by the surviving *Sonderkommando* Shlomo Dragon in March 1945 and published by the Auschwitz Museum in 1971; his second manuscript, sold by a local Pole to a Jew called Haïm Wollnerman, was published in 1977. For me, Gradowski is the most compelling, and immediate of all Shoah memoirists, and he is unbearable to read.

Still, we go on, because people write Shoah pulp fiction, and people read it.

Emil prays with Meissner.

It is not the Jewish way to kneel to pray, but Emil did so now, lowering himself onto the prie-dieu. He was unsure of what shape his prayer should take. Before his encounter with Meissner ... his life had been simple but certain. He carried the burden of Auschwitz with him everywhere and had become used to its grim companionship.

Emil knew "his life was meaningless. He raised his eyes to the figure on the cross. 'Is that it?' he mouthed silently. 'Is that how a Christian prays – by listening?' The bronze eyes stared sightlessly back at him. Emil shook his head and pushed himself up from the prie-dieu."

It worked! Emil concedes, that "he [Meissner] helped me find something precious that I thought was lost for ever". And what is that? "Myself." Meissner dies, and Emil, made whole by the encounter with a perpetrator, travels to Auschwitz to scatter his ashes and say Kaddish for him, "for all of them". At this obscenity – we are all equally victims of the Shoah – I think of a line from Lanzmann's *Shoah*. "The Jews are gone," the SS officer Franz Suchomel tells Lanzmann. "They can't tell the story anymore." Suchomel could be speaking of *The Death's Head Chess Club*, a novel he would have loved.

Donoghue has read Primo Levi: he even stole a line from him. Meissner says to Emil: "Do you remember what you once said to me in Auschwitz? 'There is no why.'" In *If This Is a Man*, Levi was thirsty and took a "fine icicle" for water. The guard snatched it. "'*Warum?*' I asked him in my poor German." The guard replied: "*Hier ist kein warum.*" (There is no why here.) The words "there is no why" were never uttered by a Jew in Auschwitz, and of all the foolish things in this foolish novel, nothing makes me angrier than this.

Donoghue's postscript reads: "I do not know whether or not there was a chess club for the SS in Auschwitz, and in my research, I have found no evidence to confirm it either way."

In 2017 Heather Morris published *The Tattooist of Auschwitz*, which incited a flurry of Auschwitz-themed novels: *The Violinist of Auschwitz* (2020); *The Midwife of Auschwitz* (2022); *The Stable Boy of Auschwitz* (2023). These are the novels John Boyne so lamented, and I think of Max Bialystock shouting: "Don't help me!"

Morris's hero – her Edward Rochester, her Justin Bieber – is the Slovakian Jew Lale Sokolov. He was – and this is true – the tattooist at Auschwitz from 1942 to 1944. There he met Gisela Fuhrmannova, a fellow prisoner: after the war they married and moved to Australia. Morris interviewed Sokolov before he died in 2006. He wanted to record his testimony so "it would never happen again". Morris published a novel eleven years later – long enough, I think, to trivialise, even forget, the man who told her his story. I call it Moon over Birkenau: Gradowski's moon, but without real grief or real love.

The book is filled with factual errors, which the Auschwitz Museum noted, and Morris does not know what good writing is. She does not have the skills to summon anything: when I read her, I see only her kitchen. Lale is a lucky Jew, ever resourceful and optimistic, and his Auschwitz is nowhere.

The prose is the dregs of romance fiction. "Her eyes dance before him." "His heart skips a beat." "His mind [is] a whirlpool." He works "around the clock". "Flowers. He learned from a young age, from his mother, that women love them." Josef Mengele, Morris's pantomime villain, has a soul "colder than his scalpel". Höss is here too: "I am in charge here at Auschwitz." ("I am completely normal.") But this is romance in hell. "I'm just a number," Gisela tells Lale. "You should know that. You gave it to me." It is also, entirely accidentally, funny. At one point someone says: "Where is everybody?" Well, quite.

Even Lale's Jewishness is – see Anne Frank's fate – an afterthought. "What they all share is fear. And youth. And their religion." "'I will not be defined by being a Jew,' Lale says. 'I won't deny it, but I am a man first, a man in love with you.'"

Twenty pages in, I am reading it as a musical: **Tattooist!**

Morris brings on a *Sonderkommando*, and snarls at him: "He too has chosen to stay alive for as long as he can, by performing an act of defilement on people of his own faith."

I think of Zalmen Gradowski, telling the *Sonderkommando*'s dreams:

His hands still feel the warmth of his child, whom he had just now held to his bosom. His wife, right here, had just been talking to him. He still remembers the content of the carefree familiar talk. Was it only a dream? And all of them, his father, mother, sisters and brothers, his wife and child – all are already long gone from this earth – burned long ago. And he is left alone here in this hellish world.

Morris, however, seems to think her fictional *Sonderkommando* should kill himself. As in – *one less life?* And yet, mere sentences later: "That the two of you [the lovers] have chosen to survive is a type of resistance to these Nazi bastards. Choosing to live is an act of defiance, a form of heroism." Which is it?

"Where are the birds?" says someone. (I forget who.) "Why aren't they singing?" That's a good point. Twenty pages in, I am reading it as a musical: *Tattooist!* I am naming the songs. It is the only way I can cope with it. I don't know if Morris means well; it barely matters. These books are so bad they are *Springtime for Hitler*'s children: they just don't know it. But, because her work was profitable, Morris opened another door.

Out flew *The Girl in the Striped Dress* (2021) by Ellie Midwood, a Jewish writer. "She refused to give up hope," says the jacket, which shows a girl facing the Birkenau guardhouse. "She dared to fall in love."

It is "a novel *mostly* based on a true story". (My italics.) In her introduction Midwood writes that in the spring of 1942, 2000 women from Slovakia were deported to Auschwitz. "Helena Citrónová" – our half-dimensional heroine – "was among them. Not long before that, a wounded *Waffen-SS* soldier, Franz Wunsch, was transferred from the Eastern Front to Auschwitz." She cites the testimony: Franz "enjoyed the girl's singing so much, he demanded that her execution be cancelled and instead signed her up to work under his command in the so-called Kanada work detail. The last names of the main characters, Helena and Franz, were changed." I will tell you why soon, because Midwood, whom I think of as a thief trailing ribbons of vapidity, dare not.

The novel opens at a Denazification tribunal in 1947, in Germany. We meet the former SS officer Franz Dahler: "A handsome face; high forehead, sharp, pleasing features, eyes – bright blue and expressive. Wavy, dark hair brushed neatly back." Franz is now married to Helena, his former slave: she accompanies him to the tribunal.

Franz is asked: "'Did you know your wife by her number only, before the liberation, as well?' 'Of course not.' Dahler chuckled." ("We are normal. We are completely normal.") "'When I learned her name, she didn't have a number yet.'"

Helena speaks: "They don't tattoo the ones who are to go into the gas chamber … And no, he never, not once, called me by my number. I was always Helena to him." Again, it only really works in song. The comic novels – this is one, though it doesn't know it – never use the real comic moments. Like the ballerina who attacked an SS man with a shoe. (Ballerinas know what shoes can do.) Or Frau Michelson, the wife of the Nazi schoolteacher at Chełmno, who appears in *Shoah*. When Lanzmann tells her 400,000 Jews were murdered at Chełmno, she simply says: "I knew it had a four in it."

Their love story is told in flashback. Helena arrives among the familiar almost-dead: "a resigned little army of shadows, already fading into nothingness". She sings for Franz; he asks for more.

"I'm afraid that will be impossible, Herr *Rottenführer*," she replies. "Our entire transport is being liquidated tomorrow … But thank you for your kind words, nevertheless. It warms my heart, knowing that I pleased you on your special day. I wish you a long and prosperous life." As no one said, ever. "I want you to exclude her from the Aktion," Franz tells her captor. A pulp god is born. "My saviour. *Rottenführer* Dahler."

Like King Lear, Helena fears madness, but in the style of a toastmaster: "I was not mad yet, or so I thought." Auschwitz "was a nightmare". One wanted "to howl, like a wolf, at the moon". Slowly, softly, Franz seduces her. Helena: "You're both murderers," she screams at Franz and his comrade, "and I'll die before I touch those hands of yours." Franz: "If you walk out of that door, I swear I'll shoot you!" I suppose marriages have been based on less.

Helena is stupid. About a fellow inmate, she muses, "Some people said he used to be a rabbi in Poland." You *are* in Poland, Helena, I scream at the page. *Auschwitz is in Poland.* Have you forgotten? To be fair, she has forgotten a lot. "Since my arrival here, I had long forgotten I was a woman and now, I suddenly remembered it and remembered that I had breasts."

The villain – despite the inevitable presence of a variant of Rudolf Höss, because no man works harder in bad novels – is not Franz, whose smiles chase "one another across his tanned face", but Novák, the *Sonderkommando*. It's an Auschwitz (love) triangle, of sorts. "You're too proud to touch my murderer's hands," shouts Franz, "but you're not too proud to touch the hands of a *Sonderkommando* pig, who drags corpses out of gas chambers daily." Not so! Helena likes Franz, because he gives her cake, and hates Novák, because he smells of death. Novák complains to the authorities about Franz's obsession with Helena, and Franz is temporarily removed, imperilling Helena's life. "Another night. Another pillow soaked with tears ... Franz!" Then, too soon: "He's back. He's back. He's back. He's back!" The reader understands. He is back.

At the tribunal, Novák accuses Franz of threatening to throw him alive into the crematorium. "[He] dragged me near the edge of the big pyre and turned me, by my collar, towards it, saying, 'Well, waste of life, tell me which I should do now – shoot you first and then throw you in there or throw you in there alive?'" Franz replies:

"I'm not trying to paint myself better than I am, but I will not sit here silently either and listen to your lies ... Besides, if we're talking about throwing people into burning pits, it's you who is guilty of this crime, not me ... Wasn't it you and your comrades who shoved an SS guard alive into the crematorium's oven during one of your revolts?"

Here, in Midwood's fiction, the SS is the saviour; the Jew, the murderer. "Let's call a spade a spade, Herr Novák. You killed an innocent man; sentenced him to die a horrific death in an oven." There is evidence this happened during the *Sonderkommando* uprising. There is no evidence it was attached to a bogus love triangle.

Back to Auschwitz, and Franz pulls Helena's sister from the gas chamber. After that, and a spate of typhus ("I don't like the way you breathe," Franz tells Helena, which makes me laugh), the romance accelerates. "Today, he brought me more bonbons. Another transport from France must have arrived." Helena is made to clean the boots of Moll, another SS officer, whose sexual tastes are more distasteful than Franz's. "No, walk over to me and kneel."

But she'll always have Franz, who is, she learns, "just an ordinary human under this uniform". She has even developed a theory that explains the rise and fall of Nazism: "I don't think your mothers hugged you enough there, in the Reich and that's the reason for all this now." Franz shares back:

> "We were to be little soldiers from the beginning … When I fell off the bicycle and twisted my ankle, my father beat me with a belt … I never cried in front of him after that. Only after he died at the front."
>
> "How old were you?"
>
> "He was killed only a year ago. So, nineteen."
>
> "No. When you fell off that bicycle."
>
> "Eight."

The mental age of the novel.

Tadeusz Borowski was a Polish political prisoner who wrote short stories based on his time at Auschwitz. I quote him to embarrass Midwood and her fictions.

> The train is emptied. We climb inside. In the corners amid human excrement and abandoned wristwatches lie squashed, trampled infants, naked little monsters with enormous heads and bloated bellies. We carry them out like chickens, holding several in each hand.

"Don't take them to the trucks, pass them on to the women," says the SS man, lighting a cigarette. His cigarette lighter is not working properly; he examines it carefully.

"Take them, for God sake!" I explode as the women run from me in horror, covering their eyes.

"What, you don't want to take them?" asks the pockmarked SS man with a note of surprise and reproach in his voice and reaches for his revolver.

"You mustn't shoot, I'll carry them." A tall grey-haired woman takes the little corpses out of my hands and for an instant gazes straight into my eyes. "My poor boy," she whispers and smiles at me.

Borowski was an honest man, and he gassed himself in 1951, six days after his daughter was born.

In *The Girl in the Striped Dress*, however, we have love, not death, and Helena and Franz have a plan: after the war they will live in Austria with a dog called Prinz in an apartment Franz looted from Jews. "If I didn't take it, someone else would have," Franz reasons, like a malfunctioning plug socket. "You know how it is. A damned sorry excuse, I know, but at least you shall live there with me and I thought that somewhat balanced things." Balanced things? After all, "Once the war is over, I will take your hand and never let it go." Is this appropriate compensation?

Back in the tribunal, Helena's sister takes the stand. "Two deep, bitter lines framed her mouth, pinched and unwilling to speak" – well, she doesn't have a Nazi to keep her warm at night.

"Would you call him a natural Jew-hater?" she is asked about Franz. "No. I would call him a very confused human being." Is she speaking about the author?

When the war ended, Helena "ran away from the Red Cross facility for displaced persons ... and searched for [Franz] until I finally found him. I slept near the barbed-wire enclosure at first. I, on one side and Franz – on the other. We held each other's hand through the fence."

By the end, even Novák is seduced by the idea of a compromised but ultimately decent Franz. "How does my seeing him only as a uniform make me different from him, who only saw all of us like vermin before someone finally came along and opened his eyes?" Maybe because he helped to murder the Jews of Europe, and you were a witness? But Novák is chastened. "I suppose I needed someone to open my eyes too. Someone has to stop this cycle of hatred. We all need to become better men."

Midwood ends with the idea that perpetrators can be redeemed if they only find the right self-help group. The psychologist – the tribunal has a psychologist – tells Franz, "You should apply for the psychiatry faculty." I goggled.

In the postscript Midwood notes what was true in her novel.

The ... development of their relationship (the love note he gave her and which she destroyed; the scene in which she refused to do his manicure for which he threatened to shoot her; the fact that he saved Helena's sister Różínka from the gas chamber; the fact that he hid Helena in the Kanada detail while she was sick with typhus and cared for her until she got better; the parcels he smuggled to her via sympathetic guards and Pipel boys; Helena and Franz's arrest after someone reported them to the camp's Gestapo; the final scene in which he gave her and her sister warm boots and instructed them on how to find his mother in Austria) are all also based on Helena's and Franz's interviews and testimonies, given to the BBC and during Franz's trial.

What she omits is this: after the war Helena rebuffed Franz's attempts to contact her, moved to Israel and married an IDF soldier. She testified at his trial in 1972, after his wife begged her, and said in an interview: "Here [in the rescue of her sister] he did something great. There were moments where I forgot that I was a Jew and that he was not a Jew and, honestly, in the end I loved him."

If the Shoah is not untellable, it is, for most people, unhearable

She said he helped her, but she also saw him abuse other prisoners. He was acquitted. There was no life together in the looted apartment in Austria; Franz didn't become a psychiatrist specialising in Jewish trauma; there was no dog called Prinz. "How completely different it would have been if we had won the war," Franz wrote in life: not with sorrow but with longing. I contacted Midwood to ask why she changed the ending. She never replied.

Midwood has already written another Auschwitz romance: *The Violinist of Auschwitz*. It earned her a rebuke from the Auschwitz

Museum: "Reading this book not only fails to enhance one's knowledge about the history of the German Nazi camp but also constructs a fabricated and deceitful image of what Auschwitz truly was, its appearance, its functioning, and the dynamics that prevailed within its walls." Its chief offence was "the description of German kapos and criminal prisoners as the architects and key participants in the camp resistance movement".

And yet, according to Gradowski, *Shoah* and other testimony, there was no such heroism. I now imagine John Boyne and Ellie Midwood, both subjects of public rebukes from the Auschwitz Museum, in a combined fiction of their own: *Novelists in Striped Pyjamas.*

The erasure of Jews from the Shoah – and the attendant malice, glibness and junk – was avoidable. If you read Gradowski and Borowski, and Wiesel and Levi, you understand quickly that the story is not untellable. Gradowski knew he wrote only "a tiny segment of the tragic world in which we lived": yet it is enough. It must be. If the Shoah is not untellable, it is, for most people, unhearable. Gradowski predicted it. In Auschwitz, he wrote, "Gradually your eye will grow blank, your heart numb, and your ears deaf."

"The Holocaust has already engendered more historical research than any single event in Jewish history," wrote the historian Yosef Hayim Yerushalmi, "but I have no doubt whatever that its image is being shaped, not at the historian's anvil, but in the novelist's crucible." This is true, and because it is true, what is remarkable is not how much authentic Shoah culture exists, but how little. It is negligible. Chava Rosenfarb's *The Tree of Life* (1985) is mostly unread. Abby Mann's *The Pawnbroker* (1964) is mostly unwatched. "You have nothing," says Mann's survivor Sol Nazerman (Rod Steiger).

> All you have is a little brain. A little brain and a great bearded legend to sustain you and convince you that you are special, even in poverty ... You are a merchant. You are known as a usurer, a man with secret resources, a witch, a pawnbroker, a sheenie, a makie and a kike!

I loved *The Brutalist* (2024) and its over-arching joke about civilisation. The non-Jew says to the Jew: build me a monument to myself! The Jew consents: he builds a concentration camp in disguise. It's a joke so good Mel Brooks could have written it.

When I think about popular Shoah culture I think of the Ariel Café in the Jewish Quarter in Cracow, where people come to experience what they think is pre-war Jewish life. There are toy Jews on the shelves – with fiddles, with Bibles, with coins – and, on the walls, paintings of Jews counting money. Ariel is, again, Jewish absence disguised as Jewish presence: when I walked in alone in 2023 and said *Shalom* to a table of Germans – to the same silence that greeted the first performance of *Springtime For Hitler* – I felt I was committing a small act of authentic Jewishness. (They did not like it. I did, very much.) Ariel is another Oz, or Primo Levi's dream in Auschwitz, "varied in its detail but uniform in its substance: they had returned home and with passion and relief were describing their past sufferings, addressing themselves to a loved person, and were not believed, indeed were not even listened to".

The dreams were true. The glut of bad Shoah culture exists because the glut is easy. In the end I think people are just too afraid to hear the truth – though this perhaps is a generous interpretation – and this is why antisemitism endures. You cannot love Jews if you refuse to understand what happened to them, and why; if you write myths around them and call it art. Still, it is what happened. We are the toys in Ariel, the ghouls in fairyland, and the rebuke to Christ. We are everywhere and nowhere; we are fictional and real.

Before John Donoghue made a Jew say Kaddish at Auschwitz for a Nazi, he stole Primo Levi's words. I will give them back to him. I end on a story from *The Truce* because I believe the truth is this: the "untouchability" of the Shoah – Borowski's "hocus pocus" and "hypnosis", Styron's "unyielding" Auschwitz, even Wiesel's admonishment of fiction ("a novel about Treblinka is either not a novel or not about Treblinka") – is a choice. Great memoirists are few – a rounding error, like rescuers – but they told their story to those who would listen, and it was testament to their genius and love of the word.

Levi's story is about a child in Auschwitz. He spoke one word, but no one knew what it meant. They called him

> Hurbinek, who was three years old and perhaps had been born
> in Auschwitz and had never seen a tree; Hurbinek, who had
> fought like a man, to the last breath, to gain his entry into the

world of men, from which a bestial power had excluded him; Hurbinek, the nameless, whose tiny forearm – even his – bore the tattoo of Auschwitz; Hurbinek died in the first days of March 1945, free but not redeemed. Nothing remains of him: he bears witness through these words of mine.

Primo Levi was civilised, and his writing is, among other things, an account of the attempt by Nazism to remove his civility, which failed. He remained himself – a Renaissance man – because "nothing is of greater vanity than to force oneself to swallow whole a moral system elaborated by others, under another sky". I don't think Levi could feel anger: he was too civilised. So he threw himself down the stairs. ≡

Works discussed

Allen, Woody (director), *Hannah and Her Sisters*, Orion Pictures, 1986

Amis, Martin, *The Zone of Interest*, Vintage, 2014

Amis, Martin, *Time's Arrow: Or the Nature of the Offence*, Harmony Books, 1991

Borowski, Tadeusz, *This Way for the Gas, Ladies and Gentlemen*, Viking/Penguin, 1946

Brooks, Mel (director), *The Producers*, Sidney Glazier, 1967

Corbet, Brady (director), *The Brutalist*, Andrew Lauren Productions/Brookstreet Pictures/Kaplan Morrison, 2024

Frank, Anne, *The Diary of a Young Girl*, translated by Anneliese Schütz, Doubleday, 1950

Gradowski, Zalmen, *The Last Consolation Vanished*, University of Chicago Press, 1977

Kramer, Stanley (director), *Judgment at Nuremberg*, United Artists, 1961

Keneally, Thomas, *Schindler's Ark*, Hodder & Stoughton (UK)/*Schindler's List*, Simon & Schuster (US), 1982

Lanzmann, Claude (director), *Shoah*, Argos Films/British Broadcasting Corporation/Les Films Aleph/Ministère de la Culture, 1985

Lanzmann, Claude, *The Patagonian Hare*, Farrar, Straus and Giroux, 2011

Levi, Primo, *If This Is a Man*, Orion Press 1947

Levi, Primo, *The Truce*, The Bodley Head, 1963

Mann, Abby, *The Pawnbroker*, Landau Company, 1964

Nemes, László (director), *Son of Saul*, Laokoon Filmgroup, 2015

Ozick, Cynthia, "The Shawl", *The New Yorker*, 1980

Ozick, Cynthia, "Who Owns Anne Frank?", *The New Yorker*, 1997

Pick-Goslar, Hannah, *My Friend Anne Frank*, Little, Brown Spark, 2023

Roth, Philip, *The Ghost Writer*, Farrar, Straus and Giroux, 1979

Spielberg, Steven (director), *Schindler's List*, Universal Pictures, 1993

Völker, Daniela (director), *The Commandant's Shadow*, Warner Bros. Pictures/Fathom Events/HBO Documentary Films, 2024

Wiesel, Elie, *Night*, Hill and Wang, 1956

The shameless list

Boyne, John, *All the Broken Places*, Doubleday, 2022

Boyne, John, *The Boy in the Striped Pyjamas*, David Fickling Books, 2006

Cavani, Liliana (director), *The Night Porter*, Lotar Film Productions, 1974

Donoghue, John, *The Death's Head Chess Club*, Atlantic Books, 2015

Hackett, Albert and Frances Goodrich, *The Diary of Anne Frank*, Random House, 1955

Littell, Jonathan, *The Kindly Ones*, HarperCollins, 2006

Midwood, Ellie, *The Girl in the Striped Dress*, Bookouture, 2021

Morris, Heather, *The Tattooist of Auschwitz*, Bonnier, 2017

Schlink, Bernhard, *The Reader*, Pantheon Books, 1995

Stevens, George (director), *The Diary of Anne Frank*, 20th Century Fox, 1959

Styron, William, *Sophie's Choice*, Random House, 1979

Sullivan, Rosemary, *The Betrayal of Anne Frank: A Cold Case Investigation*, HarperCollins, 2022

Never miss an issue.
Subscribe and save.

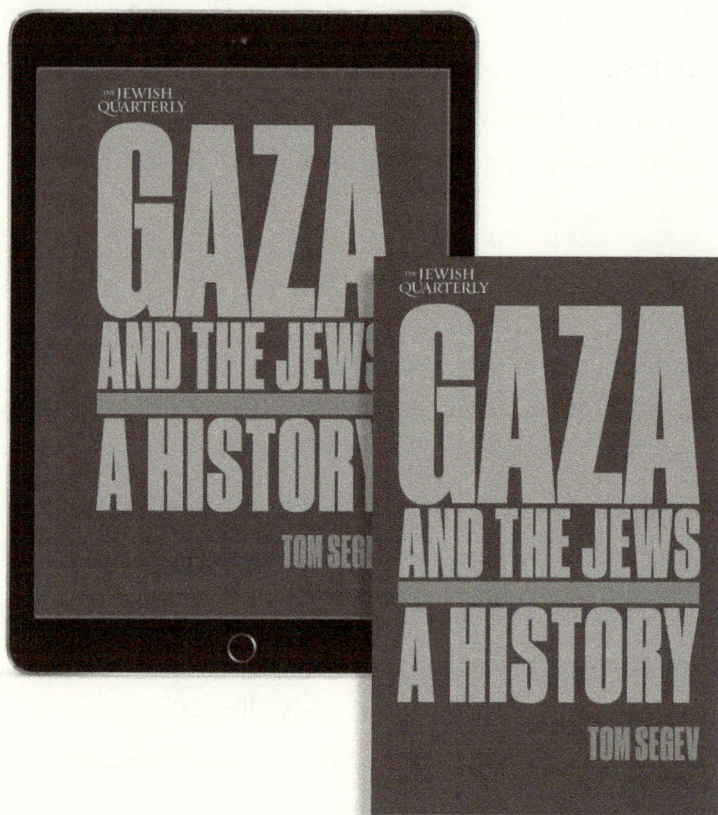

Subscribe now

- 1 year print and digital subscription (4 issues)
  £42 GBP | $56 USD | $74.99 AUD
- 1 year digital subscription (4 issues)
  £25 GBP | $32 USD | $44.99 AUD

Visit **jewishquarterly.com/subscribe**
Email **subscribe@jewishquarterly.com**

Or scan the QR code with your mobile device camera:

PART OF AN INSTITUTION? RECOMMEND JQ TO YOUR LIBRARY.
An institutional digital subscription provides students, academics and staff with access to more than 70 years of back issues, as well as each new issue as it is published. Visit our subscribe page or send us an email to learn more.

PRICES INCLUDE POSTAGE AND HANDLING.
Prices and discounts current at the time of printing. Your subscription will automatically renew until you notify us to stop. We will send you a reminder notice prior to the end of your subscription period.